INSIDE
PARKHURST

INSIDE PARKHURST

Stories of a Prison Officer

David Berridge

SEVEN DIALS

First published in Great Britain in 2021 by Seven Dials
an imprint of The Orion Publishing Group Ltd
Carmelite House, 50 Victoria Embankment
London EC4Y 0DZ

An Hachette UK Company

1 3 5 7 9 10 8 6 4 2

A CIP catalogue record for this book is
available from the British Library.

ISBN (Mass Market Paperback) 978 1 8418 8422 6
ISBN (eBook) 978 1 8418 8423 3

Typeset by Born Group
Printed and bound in Great Britain by Clays Ltd, Elcograf S.p.A.

www.orionbooks.co.uk

Dedicated to my wife,
Marilyn

CONTENTS

'Deep into that darkness peering, long I stood there, wondering, fearing'

The Raven, Edgar Allan Poe

PREFACE

Prison officers are constantly reminded that we're not privy to the bigger picture. And while that may be true, we are each privy to our own smaller picture, our experiences within the prison walls. And this is what this book is: twenty-eight years in the prison service as seen through my own eyes. Names and characteristics have been changed, including those of the constantly changing rota of staff, and dates and timelines have also been altered, but everything you'll read happened. My opinions are of course my own. The language is, as you would expect, a little colourful, the violence intense and very real. This is the unsanitised reality of an ordinary prison officer's life on the landings.

I should also point out that the stories I am telling are all taken from the time that I was in the prison service, from 1992 to 2019, and many of the terms, job titles and practices have changed since then. Throughout, I have used the language and terminology of my time.

INTRODUCTION
The Secret Service

It was the escape that did it.

On 3 January 1995, three of the prison's desperate inmates made an escape from HMP Parkhurst – inmates who were on my wing, D wing. They fashioned a home-made key, rumour had it from copying a member of staff's keys, made a ladder and even a replica gun, and, once out, only the failure of their plan to steal a plane and get off the Isle of Wight led to their capture. Although they were safely behind bars once again within five days, their escape would have severe repercussions for both the prison and the people who worked there – and the aftershock would be felt all the way up to the highest levels of government.

I had a ringside seat from which to watch the various ranks point fingers, blame each other and attempt to stitch one another up. As Jim Royle from the TV show *The Royle Family* might have said, '*Esprit de corps*, my arse.' It turned out that, rather ironically, the prison service took no prisoners when it came to covering its own. It would shaft anyone to save face and I saw good, honest, hard-working people of all ranks suffer the consequences for no other reason than that they were easy targets.

Up until then, I'd been on what I imagined was a slow but rewarding path up the ranks of the prison service. I had joined the service with every intention of making a career of it. I had envisaged a slow, steady climb through the ranks, from officer to senior officer, principal officer and then, with a bit of luck and hard work, maybe even on to governor grade. I had it all worked out and even as I sit here writing this, I'm astounded at my naivety.

That escape and its fallout sealed my future in the prison service. Not for me the back-stabbings and the cover-ups – that was a game that I simply wouldn't and most definitely couldn't play. But what I could do was take my place along the ranks of other prison officers, and do a job that was at times not only tough, terrifying and dangerous, but which was also filled with good humour, camaraderie and mutual respect – if the job was done right. And, as you'll soon see, it wasn't a job that was always done right. But it must have had something going for it, because it was a job I would continue in for another twenty-four years until I finally retired in 2019.

The prison service is very much a secret service. It exists in the shadows, away from the other major public services – the police, fire and National Health Service. How often does a political party campaign on prison reform, when they could be selling the panacea they'd provide to the NHS and to crime figures? After the crime comes the punishment, of course, but that's the part that we like to keep out of sight and out of mind.

The only time any interest is shown in the prison service is when something goes badly wrong. The fallout from the Parkhurst escape saw MP Michael Howard, Home Secretary at the time of the escape, famously squirm before the repeated questioning from Jeremy Paxman on *Newsnight* – that's how high that went. Escapes, strikes, deaths in prison are all newsworthy, but unfortunately a lot of the good stuff that is done within the prison walls goes unreported. An officer talking to and disarming a psychopath in his cell doesn't make for a headline. Saving the life of a rapist or murderer is never going to hold the front page. And preventing an escape through teamwork and intelligence gathered by switched-on officers doing a difficult job under intensely demanding circumstances just isn't on the same level as *The Great Escape*. On many occasions, the national media can't even make up their minds what our actual job title is. Wardens? Guards? Warders?

On the other side of the scale, however, are the everyday horrors that the public aren't exposed to. The suicide attempts, the blood – or claret, as we prefer to call it – the dirty protests, the violence and intimidation, the mental health issues and the desperation, the constant supply of synthetic drugs like spice filling up prisons with devastating consequences. Or the endless reams of paperwork and humdrum tick-box tasks, and trying to keep the peace at mealtimes.

But that's the life of a prison officer. It's certainly not a vocation or a calling. I've never heard anyone say, 'When I grow up, I want to be a prison officer.' I do, however, hear a lot of people say, 'How on earth did I end up being a screw?' Yet, for the first fifteen to twenty years in the job I can honestly say that I enjoyed it. The challenging nature of the job meant staff of every rank, from the governor grade to the OSG (Operational Support Grade – formerly a prison auxiliary), had a mutual respect. A respect born out of adversity. But, sadly, this respect has gradually become a thing of the past.

Staff shortages thanks to budget cuts have hit the prison service hard. These swingeing cuts, the effects of which began to be felt in 2010–11, have spiked incidences of violence, death, self-harm and drug abuse. It doesn't take a genius to see that reducing government spending on a service that has seen its inmate population rise from 44,552 in 1993 to 83,295 in 2018 is going to have consequences.

I believe these consequences to be serious. The cuts are creating a powder keg that will one day explode. Many highly experienced prison officers have left the service and cultural changes in the service means officers are now swamped with paperwork. Not only that, but the system prioritises bureaucracy and box-ticking over skills that can only be acquired through years of working on a landing and dealing with some of the most dangerous and unscrupulous criminals in the country face to face. The warning signs are there in a system stretched to breaking point but, as is my experience in the prison service, this explosion will actually have to happen before anything will be done about it.

My desire to share the unvarnished truth about life as an ordinary prison officer inspired me to write this book. The danger, the fear, the teamwork, the humour – inevitably of the black variety – the famous and infamous inmates, and the everyday incidents that we soon learn to take for granted in the job. Everything you are about to read is the truth as I saw it. This is my honest, unvarnished account of my twenty-eight years as a screw.

PART I:

Inside Parkhurst

CHAPTER I

Training

Here I was, just three weeks short of my thirty-second birthday, in prison. I'd left a perfectly good job to be here, been on the slow, steady path to promotion; my previous employer had even put me through college. But I didn't want to work in an office, and the prison service looked interesting, challenging and rewarding – so much more than just a job.

Now, as the huge wooden gates slammed shut and I stood nervously waiting, I was beginning to wonder if I'd done the right thing. I thought about the opening scene of the television sitcom *Porridge*, in which the voiceover passes judgement on Norman Stanley Fletcher, played by Ronnie Barker, as 'an habitual criminal' and imposes a sentence of five years – before the gates of the fictional HMP Slade similarly slam shut.

Shrewsbury Prison was old and it showed. A large, imposing Georgian prison first built in the late 1700s, it was affectionately known to the locals as The Dana, owing to it having been built near the site of an even older prison, the medieval Dana Gaol. All sorts of thoughts were racing through my mind in this strange environment. So alien, so oppressive and so frightening – it was like entering the underworld, a place of misery, evil, hate and condemnation. It was, for some, quite literally the end of the road.

My senses were working overtime: the smell, the noise of the gates clanging shut and reverberating. I felt like a prisoner in my desperate thoughts, but thankfully I wasn't alone.

There were five others in the same position as me, all as different as could be – a range of ages and sizes. None of them necessarily looked like I'd imagined a prison officer to look – but then I was pretty sure I didn't look like a prison officer, either. How had they ended up here and why? A question they were probably asking of themselves. I scrutinised them carefully, trying to get the measure of each of them, weighing them up. Were they reliable? Were they as nervous as I was? Could I count on them and, above all, would we survive?

So began day one of our careers as prison officers, in the obligatory two-week introduction course, a sort of 'try before you buy' taster to gain a feel for what it was like to be 'inside'. We had entered together and I hoped that we would get through this fortnight together.

When two prison officers eventually collected us, they looked pretty pissed off. Was it us? Or was that just what the job did to you? But we had little time to dwell on such thoughts, as we were inducted rapidly through the rules and regulations, and given our timetable for the next two weeks, which would always begin with a morning gym session. And we were presented with large blue notebooks, which we were instructed to fill out daily as a record of the day's events.★

Each day we would visit a new section – the reception, segregation unit (Seg unit), the wings, healthcare (HCC), library, workshops – where we would observe, take notes,

---

★ The contents of these notebooks, over the years, would form the basis of this book.

ask numerous stupid questions, get in the way and stick out like sore thumbs. If there was a problem or we heard an alarm bell, we were to remain where we were and not get involved. That was absolutely fine by me.

In our jackets and ties, hopelessly out of our depth, we did indeed stick out. We were easy targets. Sink or swim. Was this a deliberate ploy? I quickly realised that one of the skills required for self-preservation in the prison environment is the ability to blend in, look calm and act as if you know what you are doing. But it was a different world. Though I stand at over six feet tall and have always considered myself very capable of looking after myself on Civvy Street, the truth was that I was now shitting myself.

After surviving the first two weeks at HMP Shrewsbury, we spent a further nine weeks at the prison service training college at Newbold Revel, an impressive eighteenth-century country estate in Warwickshire. Training was split between classroom and practical lessons – with Control and Restraint (C & R), an approved technique for officers to control a violent, aggressive inmate physically – taking up much of this. This wasn't just manhandling a violent inmate to the ground; it was a technique using wrist locks and other methods adopted from martial arts, which had to be perfected through practice. I'd always been capable of looking after myself, but this was something else entirely – a technique that required mastery. Our fitness levels were monitored and regular tests were set in both the theory and the practical. Having not signed up to join the military, I hadn't counted on the almost daily marches that we would be subjected to.

The many ex-military types among us included squaddies, sailors, bootnecks (Royal Marines) and the RAF, who fortunately were only too happy to help those of us who had never marched anywhere or were born with two left feet. Some trainees were former prison auxiliaries* who had decided to become prison officers and, having a basic understanding of how the prison worked (though they didn't work directly with any inmates), they were thankfully more than happy to answer any silly questions. It seemed everyone had a particular skill to share and, despite thinking I didn't, a spell in the merchant navy as a deckhand had given me a grasp of the Phonetic Alphabet, which we were tested on.

Towards the end of the course we had to choose the prison where we wished to work. We had to provide three choices and we were by no means certain to get our first preference. I chose HMP Parkhurst, for a simple reason: its notoriety meant that it was one of the very few prisons I had even heard of. It housed the most dangerous, violent offenders in the country: gangsters, psychopaths, terrorists – the mad, the bad and the just plain evil. Funnily enough, Parkhurst was always crying out for new officers, so those of us who chose it got our first choice.

At the end of our nine weeks at Newbold Revel, there was no time to recover, gather our thoughts or sort out minor details like moving the family down to the new prison, or even finding out exactly where the prison was. I lived just outside Shrewsbury at the time with my wife and would have to relocate entirely to the Isle of Wight. We finished on the Friday and started work on the Monday – though it would be another couple of weeks before we were let loose on any actual prisoners.

---

* Later known as Operational Support Grade (OSG).

CHAPTER 2

The Rats' Nest

Day one

We arrived at HMP Parkhurst bright and early. There were five of us NEPOs (New Entrant Prison Officer) from the training school and it was a relief to see some familiar faces. Not that anyone would ever let on: we all fronted it out and tried to look confident. Our principal officer (PO), the highest uniformed rank, laid it out straight from the beginning: 'Forget all that crap they taught you at the school. None of it bears any resemblance to real prison life and none of it will be of any use to us here.'

I was fortunate indeed in this respect, as so little of what we had supposedly learnt had really sunk in anyway. In truth, the real training was only now about to start.

The looming gloomy brick buildings of Parkhurst had housed some of the most dangerous prisoners in the land and its location on the Isle of Wight provided a double lock of security. Even if a con escaped the prison walls, they would then have a stretch of water to mainland England to navigate – or the English Channel if they tried for France.

Parkhurst had a long and dark history. First opened in 1838 as a prison for young male offenders, it briefly became a temporary home to female convicts in 1863 to 64, until 1869, when it became the prison for male offenders it remained to this day. Parkhurst courted controversy from the beginning for its particularly tough regime, and its reputation grew during the twentieth century. In 1968, it became one of the first dispersal prisons for maximum-security offenders, housing category A prisoners★ in a special secure unit (SSU) – an extra-secure prison within an already highly secure prison. There were several SSUs throughout the country to allow category A prisoners to be dispersed.

This prison within a prison at Parkhurst had at one time or other been home to inmates like Charles Bronson, Donald Neilson (the Black Panther), the Krays, the Brink's-Mat robbers, Valerio Viccei (mastermind of the £60 million Knightsbridge Security Deposit robbery in 1987), and terrorists like Hindawi (who in April 1986 attempted to plant a bomb on a flight from London to Tel Aviv using his unwitting innocent Irish fiancée to carry the explosive device on board the flight) as well as members of the IRA.

In short, it was an intimidating, forbidding place. But it was in a state of change. The whole prison was actually a building site, with two wings out of action while they were being brought up to date and to category A standard. Things like internal sanitation – toilets in each of the cells – were being installed, while the old, flammable wooden floors and cell doors were being replaced. Sprinklers, tannoy systems, new hotplates and a host of mod cons to make the place escape-proof were being added to this Victorian relic.

We were new officers, in a new prison, wearing new uniform, and we looked exactly what we were: *new*, clueless and out of our depth. The PO informed us that we were

---

★ Categories ranged from A to D, with A the most secure/high risk prisoners and D those who pose the least threat and have open conditions.

to spend a fortnight going through an induction process. We'd see how things were really done and why.

The basic things were made clear from the start.

Don't ever show your keys. Conversations between each other must be out of earshot. Never pass stuff between inmates. (Inmates would often ask for a newspaper or magazine to be passed, or say something like, 'Guv, can you give this to so and so on your wing when you see him' – all no-nos.) Grooming, manipulation and/or conditioning. (Inmates would try to condition you into thinking a certain way, through saying things like, 'Don't touch that, Guv, it's from my kids', or, 'We don't do this, we go over there', when being escorted.) The use of the emergency alarm bells. Fire alarms. Radio procedure. Red phones. Wing and workshop evacuation. Don't fuck these things up. My head was spinning already. And then we visited the wings.

We started with B wing, known as the Rats' Nest: 132 inmates, five landings and a reputation for being possibly the most dangerous building in the UK. Thankfully, one thing that had stuck during training was the naming of the landings: 'the ones' referred to the ground floor, 'the twos' the first floor and so on. But nothing in our training had quite prepared us for this.

The smell of a prison wing is unique, a powerfully pungent aroma of cleaning products, stale body odour, fear, urine and faeces. And then there's the cacophony of noise, inmates shouting to one another between cells, at officers, and all manner of banging and clattering reverberating around the place. The suicide netting, the prison officers who gave off an air of authority and competence we NEPOs could surely never hope to attain, the austere doors and walkways – it was terrifying and yet strangely exciting.

Next up, C wing special unit. This was where those who were too dangerous to be housed in places like Broadmoor, the high-security psychiatric hospital in Berkshire, resided. The criteria for an inmate to be admitted to Broadmoor was that they must be deemed to be curable or benefit from the therapeutic regime. If they were beyond any chance of help or cure, however, C wing was where they ended up. This wing was a national resource and held what Hollywood would no doubt call the criminally insane. So dangerous were the inmates housed here that there was a multidisciplinary team with a resident psychiatrist, psychologists and hospital officers responsible for the administering of the prescribed medication – medication that we all hoped kept them subdued, relatively sane or quiet.

We finished the tour in the segregation unit (the Seg unit) – known variously as the block or chokey – which was basically the punishment block. Any inmate whose behaviour demanded their removal from the regular wing would be taken here, where they would be segregated from other prisoners. We were informed that the Seg unit screws had to volunteer to work here and be accepted by the other officers, as the job involved dealing with inmates at their worst and needed a tight crew.

The one unit that we were not allowed in was the protected witness unit (PWU) – or, as the media would prefer, the supergrass unit. Each inmate had a price on his head for having turned supergrass. So secure was this unit that the inmates left their names behind when they were located here and were identified only as a Bloggs: Bloggs 1, Bloggs 2 and so on. They had a security system so tight that even if the governor tried to gain access, he would be dismissed unless it was by prior arrangement or the necessary phone calls granting clearance had been made.

There was so much to take in, my head was once again spinning by the end of the day.

The great escape

When I turned up for work this morning I was, along with every other member of staff, told to report to the visits area, where all the full staff meetings were held. We were briefed about last night's attempted escape, where three inmates had apparently dug their way through the walls and out of their cells. They had removed a number of the old Victorian bricks and were in the process of making good their escape. However, they were apparently so busy arguing among themselves that they had inadvertently alerted the staff. As one officer put it, 'They'd made enough frigging noise to wake the dead.' Planning and teamwork was, fortunately, not the would-be escapers strongest point and they were caught red-handed. Now located in the block (the Seg unit), they were due to be shipped out to another dispersal prison.

Preparing for battle

The remaining week and a half of training went by in a bit of a blur. Talk about sensory overload: the noise, smell, language, rules, dos and don'ts, the geography and layout of the place . . . Parkhurst was like a maze – now I knew how prospective London cabbies must have felt learning the Knowledge. The trouble was that if I was escorting inmates, I obviously couldn't ask them which way to go.

I couldn't ask an officer, because he would either think me clueless, or deliberately give me the wrong directions. If there was an alarm bell situation, I wouldn't be able to run – sorry, attend 'post-haste', as officially you aren't supposed to run to an alarm bell – to where I was going. I had to learn so many things, and learn fast.

Tomorrow would be my first shift on an actual wing. It would only be for three hours of an ED (evening duty), but at least I would be on the wing as a proper prison officer. To say I was a little apprehensive would be an understatement. I had unfortunately made the mistake of listening to some of the long-serving officers, whose war stories of battles fought on the landings were like someone's granddad recounting their good fortune to have survived the First World War trenches. I remembered part of Tennyson's 'The Charge of the Light Brigade'.

> Boldly they rode and well,
> Into the jaws of death,
> Into the mouth of hell.

A little dramatic, maybe, but hey, I was crapping myself. If this wasn't the time for high drama then when was?

The next day

I turned up at a little before 18.00 this evening and reported to the wing office. If I'd thought for one single moment that I was going to be welcomed with open arms, I would have been sadly mistaken. I was about as welcome as a turd in a swimming pool. I introduced myself and explained that I had been told to report here. Without so much as a 'Hello, how are you? What's your name? Would you like a cup of tea? Welcome to B wing,' I was simply asked, 'Have you got a radio?' And when I replied that I hadn't, the response was immediate: 'Well, you'd better get one. You're Juliet 6.' Whatever the hell Juliet 6 was. I made my way to the gate, collected the radio and asked what I had to do as Juliet 6. The answer was as immediate as it was unhelpful: 'You'll find out.'

I had walked into an ambush. My colleagues had obviously eyed me up and decided that I wasn't really worth the effort until I'd proven myself in the heat of battle. I expected the inmates to give me the runaround, fuck me about and generally make my life as unpleasant and as difficult as possible. But the reality of working on a wing as a NEPO was that the longer-serving, well-established prison officers were far more frightening than any of the inmates. They were understandably unsure, untrusting and wary of me.

We worked in one of the most dangerous places in the country. Officers needed to be able to trust and count on each other in such a volatile and violent environment. I was an unknown quantity; I hadn't yet earned the right to be liked or accepted.

Thankfully, one young officer came over and explained that I was to 'join the net' and collect prisoners for the gym session, then escort them to the gym. There were, however, several problems with this seemingly simple task. How did I collect prisoners? How did I join the net? And how the hell did I escort them? I was just so grateful that someone had actually spoken to me that I'd forgotten to ask.

My radio training at Newbold Revel seemed like a dim and distant memory, but I somehow fumbled my way through a test call to ensure the radio was working and establish that I was now Juliet 6, the officer responsible for escorting the gym party to and from the gym. I had 'joined the net' (the radio network). Each job within the prison had its own separate call sign. For example, Mike unit was the officer responsible for the classes/education; Zulus were the dog handlers, Oscars the POs, Victors the various governors; Kilos were the Seg unit officers and Hotels were hospital officers.

The wing had been unlocked, so all of the inmates were milling around.★ I knew that I needed to look and sound confident in front of my colleagues, while at the same time convincing the inmates that I wasn't actually in need of a pair of adult-size Pampers nappies. So I shouted at the top of my faltering voice, 'Gymnasium!' Self-confidence and voice projection would require some work, that much was clear. But somehow I managed to pull it off, because no sooner had the last syllable left my very dry mouth than I was inundated with thirty to forty inmates, all chomping at the bit and keen to get to the gym.

It was only when I got on the radio to ask permission to move to the gym that I learnt I could only take sixteen inmates. Shit. Yet another trap. Which sixteen? I was in a bit of a pickle, so I stood at the gate and only let one inmate out at a time, counting as they went. This was nowhere near as easy as you might think. If they weren't grunting, growling or swearing, they were throwing in the odd thirty-one, forty-nine, eleven, seventeen, all designed to throw my counting out. Count discreetly: another lesson learnt.

When I reached the last of the sixteen, I went to close the gate, which was a bit like trying to remove a hungry Rottweiler's meal while he's still eating. Despite the growling,

---

★ I didn't realise then that the gym was first come, first served.

grunting, snarls and threats – and my shaking, slippery-with-sweat hands – I finally got the gate secured. I then *discreetly* tried to catch up with the inmates, whom I really hoped were walking in the right direction and not taking me on some wild goose chase. I had a quick recount, *discreetly* double-checking that I had the sixteen who I had left the wing with, while trying to look as nonchalant and relaxed as I could.

Zulu units – or should I say the dog handlers – were strategically located along the route. The dogs were watching the inmates with great interest and the handlers were no doubt watching me with even greater interest. It was only when we reached another set of gates that I thought I might be rumbled, trying to unlock gates with still-shaking hands while trying to discreetly work out which key was the right one.

I was met by a couple of PEIs (physical education instructors, who were prison officers who had trained for this role) in the gym. It was then a case of signing the various cat A books★ that had just been delivered by the wing cleaning officer (responsible for feeding the inmates, checking on the wing cleaners to ensure they are doing the cleaning to a satisfactory standard, making sure the wing storeroom is stocked and delivering the cat A books to where they are needed and locating the inmates). I was then shown into the observation area, a small, secure room from which I could watch the inmates and, if need be, safely raise the alarm.

★ Cat A books are similar to the old blue passports: wherever a category A prisoner goes the cat A book must follow him. It's a record of a cat A's movement and must be signed by the receiving area.

Watching the inmates train with weights and punchbags, I was glad that I was locked in this small, secure room out of harm's way. It was the law of the jungle in there, an alpha male exhibition of physical prowess and machismo. A bunch of pissed-off, testosterone-fuelled killers – towering of ego and surging with adrenaline – refusing to display even a hint of weakness. And the atmosphere in there fizzed with the very real sense that just the one misread signal, one small infringement of gym etiquette, was all it would take for the whole place to explode.

Once the prisoners had had their hour-long session, the whole process was repeated in reverse. I radioed for permission to move back to the wing, with sixteen pumped-up inmates, including the eleven 'packages'. 'Package' was the term used for a cat A prisoner.

Only when the Zulu units were in place could I secure permission to move back to the wing. As I handed in the cat A books, I was relieved not to have fucked up my first job. I was told I was on·the fives, so I duly went and stood on the landing on my own until 'bang up' (which is locking-up time) at 21.15. I could see other officers and they occasionally glanced at me, as did the inmates, weighing me up, checking me out. I tried my best to look relaxed, but I was sneaking glances at my watch every few minutes, while my face felt bright red, my heart was racing and my knuckles were turning white, which I realised was simply because I was gripping the railings a little too tight. I was holding on for dear life.

First blood

At last. Today was my first full day as a prison officer. When I arrived I was told to 'get the kettle on'. As was apparently the tradition, the NEPOs made the brews and, not wanting to fuck up something that simple to start with, off I went with my scrap of paper with their orders: tea, a splash of milk and two sugars; coffee, lots of milk and no sugar; coffee, black, none . . . However, before I even made it to the kettle, a cell bell sounded, which was quickly followed by shouts from the office: 'Bell on the fives!' Another apparent tradition: send the NEPO up to answer the cell bell.

I made my way up the stairs and onto the fives landing. The little red cell–bell light above the door on cell six was illuminated, so I slid the observation flap open and was greeted with what appeared to be a living Jackson Pollock painting.

The walls, ceiling and floor were decorated with what seemed, at first glance to my inexperienced eyes, to be red paint. It was only when I spotted the inmate slumped in the corner that I realised it was claret (blood). He was holding his throat with both hands and both of his arms had long, deep lacerations running from wrist to elbow. His thighs were also cut deeply and bleeding profusely.

I couldn't believe what I was seeing. I shut the flap, gathered my thoughts and tried to take it in, then opened the observation flap for a second look. *Bollocks, bollocky bollocks.* It was real, very fucking real. Now, my mind went into overdrive. What had they taught me at Newbold Revel? I tried to remember – it was in there somewhere . . .

Do I open the door and possibly save his life? *No.*

Do I hit the general alarm so that every man and his dog will know what is going on? *No.*

Do I shout down to my colleagues, who were still waiting for their tea, and wake up the whole wing? *No.*

Do I run down four flights of stairs and explain what is going on, or what I think is going on? *Yes.*

I raced down, tried desperately to calm myself and then explained to the other officers that it looked like the inmate in cell six on the fives had cut his throat because there was blood everywhere. (I was a bit non-committal, because I still couldn't quite believe what I had seen.)

Things happened very quickly from there. The prison hospital was contacted, Oscar 1 (O1), the call sign for the PO in charge – was summoned, all and any available staff and Zulu units turned up, and two other officers and I returned to the cell to administer first aid. The floor of the cell was both slippery and sticky with blood, and as soon as we moved the inmate for a closer inspection, an arterial spray hit both me and the ceiling – I was now covered in claret. One of the officers tried to staunch the flow by pressing a towel onto the wound, while the other collected some blankets and towels to put on the slippery floor so we could work without sliding around. I wrapped the inmate's arms and thighs in towels.

My white shirt was now red, and my hands looked like they were encased in red gloves and felt like they had been dipped in treacle. There was sticky, smelly blood every-where. I held towels on his legs in a desperately feeble effort to look as if I was actually doing something useful. My colleague appeared to be strangling the inmate in an attempt to stop the flow of blood from his neck wound and then, after what seemed like an eternity, the cavalry arrived. A couple of hospital officers arrived – the 'scab lifters', as they were affectionately known – and took over. No rush, no panic; they calmly assessed the situation and, before doing anything else, put their gloves on.

Fuck! We had been told and told in training that inmates are prone to carrying all sorts of unpleasant things: hepatitis, HIV, STDs, tetanus and God knows what else. 'Before

22

you deal with injuries or wounds you must always, always put your gloves on,' was the advice. We also had to have various jabs and yet all this advice went out of the window the moment we entered the cell. The fact that the other two officers hadn't put gloves on made me feel a little better. I really hoped the inmate didn't have any of these dreaded lurgies.

Rivalling with these fears was another thought: How did I do? Did I cock it up? Would I get a bollocking? Thankfully, the wing senior officer (SO) took me to one side and reassured me that I 'did the right thing', which was further confirmed when the number one governor of the prison came onto the wing and asked how I was, stating that in all probability my quick thinking had saved the inmate's life.* But the real confirmation that I'd done all right arrived in the form of action: when I had a cup of tea actually made for me by a *proper officer*.

Slippery inmates

Unlocking the wing required two officers per landing. One officer unlocked every cell on one side of the landing, while the other officer did the other side. There was one inmate in each cell, and prior to unlocking, both officers would make sure the number of inmates was correct. I was on one side of the landing today, trying to unlock cell doors and look all slick and professional, when I realised that the officer unlocking the other half of the landing had already finished and was now watching my rather feeble fumblings. No pressure, then.

---

* About a year later the inmate would make a successful attempt on his life, hanging himself.

He suddenly turned sharply and disappeared into a cell a few doors away from him, then reappeared and beckoned me over. An inmate had collapsed and he had a small cut just above his left eye. As I walked in, I nearly went arse over tit on the slippery floor. We grabbed him and put him on his bed. He was coherent and chatty, refusing point-blank to have any further help or let the healthcare centre (HCC) take a look at the wound on his head.

When we asked him what had happened, he explained that he had been constipated for several days and one of the other inmates had assured him that the best way to cure constipation was with baby lotion. 'Squirt the stuff up your jacksey, two or three times a day, and that will sort it,' was the non-expert advice. He'd got a little too enthusiastic with sticking it up his bottom and squirting, so he'd spilled a load on the floor and slipped on it, banging his head. We never did find out if it actually cured his constipation.

Meal times

The hotplate was basically a servery, where inmates lined up and collected their meals, which they would then take back to their cells to eat. When I was informed that I was to man the hotplate, I assumed I would be there in some sort of supervisory capacity, strategically standing to one side and looking all mean and menacing lest an inmate decide to misbehave or dare to complain about the custard having lumps in it. I was, or so I thought, there to act as a deterrent. Wrong. I would be, along with half a dozen other officers, actually serving the inmates their meal.

The other staff were already in place, so I grabbed the only available space left: the chips. I was given a brief, somewhat sarcastic, lesson on how to use the J611 Flat-Handled Chip Scoop, a screw-proof implement for the serving of chips, accompanied with dire warnings of 'Don't run the fuck out of chips.' Only then were we good to go.

The cleaning officer was overseeing the whole operation and would give each inmate a number, which corresponded to his food. This number was shouted out for each inmate, though it certainly didn't help that I didn't yet know a single inmate's name.

As the inmates slowly came through, I was impressed with the speed and dexterity of the whole operation. The only problem area seemed to be mine. I was a nervous wreck again. One scoop per inmate, it wasn't exactly rocket science, but here I was, convinced I was giving out the wrong amount of chips. I was grunted at, moaned at and given the evil eye by the inmates. I looked longingly over to the cabbage and peas section. It was a world away from the poisoned chalice that was the chips.

Invisible intruder

The cell bells are only ever to be used in an emergency. Or at least that's the theory. To a prison officer, an emergency is a life-or-death situation. Like the prisoner cutting his own throat. But after only a week in the job, I'd learnt that a prisoner has a slightly different definition: running out of toilet paper, a cockroach walking across the floor, a headache, the sound of voices, real or imagined. Last night, three staff were called to a cell in another wing because an inmate had pressed the cell bell at 02.20, then started shouting and kicking the door. He woke some of the other inmates, and a domino effect saw the shouts of 'shut the fuck up' and 'wait till I see you in the morning' rise to a crescendo.

A dog handler was called and O1 was asked to attend after getting no verbal response from the inmate, who was too busy shouting and screaming, and who could be seen cowering in the corner of his cell while trying to protect himself with a pillow from an apparently invisible assailant. When the staff finally entered the cell and the inmate eventually calmed down enough, he explained that there was a wasp in the cell and he was allergic to wasps.

Psychological torment

Today, the head psychologist came looking for me and asked if he could have a quiet word, and now I was shitting myself, again. Have I fucked up? What have I done? What haven't I done? What should I have done? Have my colleagues already decided that there's no place in the service for a bloke who can't even make a decent cup of tea? And, Will I ever stop shitting myself?

My self-deprecating thoughts of total inadequacy were interrupted when we sat down together in his office and he proceeded to ask if I was OK. I must have looked a little bemused, because he then said, 'I understand you were the one who found Doyle, the inmate with the cut throat. I understand that it was a bit messy, so I thought I'd come and see if you are all right and, if it's OK, could I ask you a couple of questions?'

I didn't mind and besides, I didn't really have much choice. The first question was: 'What did you think about what you had to deal with?' The million-dollar question.

This caught me slightly off guard. Did I tell the truth and say that I hadn't given the incident a second thought, as I'd been too busy trying to survive each and every subsequent shift? And have the psychologist decide I was a cold-hearted, uncaring, ruthless bastard who displayed a lack of empathy towards another human being. Or did I say I'd thought about it a lot and could only hope that the inmate was OK, and that yes, there was a lot of blood? Which made me feel a little uneasy, the psychologist potentially deciding that I wasn't mentally strong enough to be working in such a demanding environment. Dilemma, dilemma.

So I did what I normally do in such situations. I bluffed my way out of it, saying I had since thought about the incident and hoped that I did the right things, and that I was just glad that Doyle was unsuccessful in his apparent suicide attempt and that my colleagues were able to prevent what could so easily have been a suicide. It worked – well, I think it worked. He seemed satisfied with my response. However, the real truth of the matter was that I was just relieved I hadn't fucked up in front of my colleagues.

Cold-blooded vertebrates

This morning we reported to the visits area, where we were briefed about a spin.* Carl, the security SO giving the speech in his strong Geordie accent, informed us that it was an intelligence-led search and that we would be looking for 'hooch' and 'amphibians'. Hooch, I knew, was illicitly brewed alcohol, but I didn't understand the term 'amphibians' and hadn't the bottle to ask, lest I looked even

---

* The prison term for a search.

more stupid than I felt, even if the chances of us having to look for cold-blooded vertebrates seemed unlikely.

Luckily, someone had the balls to raise their hand and ask the question. Carl's accent seemed to become broader the more excited he got. Being one of those people whose mouth seemed to work faster than their brain, he explained that what he actually meant was 'amphetamines'. The whole place erupted.

After the meeting, we made our way to the wings. Wing officers rarely search their own wings during a complete wing spin, so we B-wing officers made our way to M wing and vice versa. I was teamed up with Clive, an experienced officer who asked me the obvious question, 'Have you done many searches?'

I was reminded of the old saying that you should never ask a question unless you know the answer. It must have been blatantly obvious to all and sundry that I was brand new and clueless. When I told him that this was to be my first, the look of disappointment in his face was obvious. He might as well have said, 'How did I end up with the fucking idiot NEPO? Why me?'

I, however, was keen to impress. I'd show him what I had learnt about searching. If there was anything to find, I'd find it all right. Clive approached the cell, gave a quick look through the spy hole, opened the door and shot the bolt.*)

---

* This is done so that the cell door can't shut fully, which would, in turn, lock the door, leaving an officer banged up in a cell. On the rare occasions that this has happened, the officer has a couple of ways of getting out. If he has a radio, he can contact the control room and ask for assistance, or he can ring the cell bell.

Clive informed the inmate that we were to do a cell search and asked the standard questions: Is everything in here yours? Have you got anything that you shouldn't have? Is there anything that is likely to harm us? Only when we were satisfied with the answers could we proceed.

The inmate was to be strip-searched, so I asked him to stand facing me and remove his T-shirt, which was searched. Then he was asked to lift his arms and turn round so we could check his armpits (an ideal hiding place). Satisfied that nothing was hidden on his top half, the T-shirt was handed back and he put it on. Socks and trousers were removed and searched. Soles of the feet were checked, in case an item was hidden under the arches of the feet. Underpants were then dropped to the knees and shaken. Occasionally, if there was reason to, an officer would ask the inmate to lift his ball bag (his scrotum), which was often used to hide things behind or beneath. I know this sounds a little extreme and somewhat degrading, but only in the outside world. In prison it's the norm. Things have been found beneath foreskins, up rectums and even in babies' nappies during visits.

Once we were satisfied that there was nothing hidden on or about his person, the inmate put his clothes back on. We asked if he had any legal papers he wanted to take out with him, which would be searched first. He didn't, so he was asked to wait outside the cell while we commenced the search. He stood outside, watching intently.

I started on the left and Clive on the right, searching from top to bottom. I methodically searched the shelves, the top of the shelves, under and behind. I found nothing.

Either way, it's a matter of some embarrassment for the officer and a source of much amusement for his or her colleagues.

Opening the small wooden locker, I carefully removed a slop bucket, which is a normal domestic plastic bucket with a lid, normally used for washing smalls or as a paper bin. This one was full of dirty washing-up water, so I replaced the lid and put the thing behind me. I carried on searching, determined to find something, anything.

Clive then asked what appeared to me to be a silly question: 'What's in the bucket?'

'Washing,' I replied. And then a little less certainly: 'I think.'

Clive lifted the lid and kindly explained that it wasn't washing. It was, in fact, hooch. And this wasn't an incy-wincy, piddly little amount of hooch but a bucketful of the stuff. The guilty party standing outside the cell couldn't stifle it any more and let out a hysterical cackle at my incompetence. Clive was fuming. I was now officially 'a fucking clueless idiot'.

The official policy for finding hooch was to place the inmate on report. He would then be hauled up in front of the governor and found guilty. It was just a question of how guilty he would be.

However, the far more effective unofficial way, I learnt later, is to give the guilty inmate an option. Be nicked or dispose of it down the recess drain. This hurts, and hurts a lot. The pained expression on the inmate's face as he tips the hooch away is always worth it. Plus, some inmates are holding it or brewing it as part of some payment plan with another inmate. And when the hooch goes missing there will often be repercussions. Clive and I, of course, did the right, official thing – only because I was new and an unknown quantity who couldn't yet be trusted.

Control and Restraint

Three weeks in and the SO informed me that I was going to be given a specific job. All officers have specific jobs and mine was to be one of the cleaning officers. This was a job that came with a lot of responsibility, from paying the wing cleaners-cum-orderlies (who were inmates), to making sure they were doing their jobs correctly, organising the diets for the 130-plus inmates on the wing,★ making sure the wing stores were up to date and feeding the inmates, which included standing on the hotplate servery area with a meal board, reading off the names and diet of each and every inmate. In other words, I needed to learn the names of all 130 plus inmates, which was never going to be easy when they refused to engage with me.

This particular morning I was on the twos, taking it all in. I watched Jimmy B going into the servery. He was one of the few inmates whose name I knew, made easy by the fact that he was on crutches, which he used to walk with, point with or hit with. He had absolutely no use of his legs, yet this apparently hadn't stopped him from being an armed robber.

An almighty commotion suddenly erupted on the ones, just below me. Milk, food, plastic cups, bowls and cutlery sent flying to the tune of angry, incoherent shouts – and then there was a sickening thud. I had a bird's-eye view of the two white shirts (prison officers) appearing and one

---

★ Each inmate chooses their meal a week in advance by filling out a short weekly menu; the cleaning officer collates this and informs the kitchen of the numbers of each diet/meal.

of them stepped over the now prone body of one of the wing cleaners, seemingly to protect him from further harm.

The inmate who had dropped him tried to continue his attack on the comatose cleaner, so I raced down the stairs and within seconds, the other officer and I were wrestling the attacker, who was now in a blind rage, spitting and spewing a venomous tirade of abuse. He was strong, a regular gym user with a history of violence and murder. He was fighting with a ferocity I had never seen before. We somehow managed to get him off balance and onto the floor.

Two other officers appeared and I think I heard the alarm go off, closely followed by the reassuring sound of the troops arriving. Now that we had the assailant on the floor, the difficult bit began. What the hell do I do? I tried hard to remember my C & R training: terms like 'goose neck', 'triangular fix', 'outward rotation', 'figure of four' and 'lock on'. So much information . . . So I did what I normally do: watched the other officer. He had control of the attacker's right arm and I barely had hold of his left – but now, as I watched, some of it was coming back to me, even as I fumbled for control. I was tapped on the shoulder and told to slow down, take my time. I watched the other officer put a final wrist lock – a hold that is used to immobilise the arm using a pain-compliance martial arts technique – on the inmate and I slowly copied. It wasn't easy, it wasn't pretty and it wasn't 'controlled and clinical' as it had been in training, but once I had a good wrist lock, I was reminded to say, 'Lock on', if I was happy I had complete control of the wrist. Once I said it, and despite the inmate still wanting to fight, two other officers took over.

As my heart rate came back down from the stratosphere, I found my overriding emotion was relief. I hadn't got hurt and I had finally experienced a real-life C & R situation. To my colleagues I'm sure it was just another day at the office, but to me it was a major step forwards, a rite of passage, even. I hadn't frozen: I got stuck in and I hadn't made a pig's ear of it. It was not only another step in the right direction, but also a confidence booster.

Trouble brewing

When I arrived on the wing at lunchtime, I checked the 'obs' book (wing observation book, for recording anything of interest that has happened on the wing). There had been a bit of a scrap on the compound – the large exercise area and also a main thoroughfare for the inmates going to and from work – between a couple of inmates who were now in the block.

After unlock, the wing sprang to life and, as usual, the cleaners got stuck into whatever mischief cleaners get up to. Inmates were called down and sent to their places of work, education or the gym, and once this was done, we banged up the unemployed and those not required owing to medical call-ups and the like. We put the kettle on, and a couple of officers commented on the wing and its atmosphere. I hadn't noticed anything out of the ordinary, but they were saying it was bubbly, which meant that there was tension, where something was bubbling just below the surface and there was possibly going to be trouble. Something as out of the ordinary and yet as simple as an inmate going into the cell of another he never normally visited, and the whole dynamic of the wing changed. The wing is a bit like a cook's ingredients, they said. Get the mixture right and everything is fine and lovely; get the mixture slightly wrong and it's fucking chaos.

The scent of danger

Today, one of the wings very nearly went up. Though the inmates were banged up, they were told that there would be a delay in unlock. They started banging the doors, making threats of violence . . . but somehow the individual door kicking and banging morphed into one unified sound – all of the inmates were working together. Individuals or pairs acting alone are at least controllable. But when the whole wing works together as one complete entity, it's frightening. This was when the wing was at its most dangerous.

The banging of doors continued for far longer than normal and had the potential to escalate, so the decision was made to bring in the dogs. Half a dozen angry, aggressive, barking Alsatians were impressive and the acoustic properties of the wing meant it acted like an echo chamber. It was a formidable, ferocious sound. The inmates hate the dogs at the best of times and when they feel threatened by the animals, they tend to quieten down. The handlers wound the dogs up so much that the barking reached fever pitch, and with the warnings about sending the dogs in and relocating a few of the inmates, there were soon only three or four determined door kickers left.

Once the decision was taken to unlock the wing, there was obviously a degree of trepidation. It was still a potentially volatile situation. Had the inmates actually calmed down, or were they still wound up? We wouldn't know until the doors were opened. Thankfully, on this occasion they had calmed down.

Alf, one of the longer serving officers, wore a rueful smile as he said that the time to worry wasn't when they were making loud threatening noises, but when they were making no noise. 'It's like the self-harmers,' he said. 'The serious ones don't make a song and dance about it and certainly don't advertise the fact. The one who genuinely wants to kill himself will be the inmate you least suspect.'

Crap on demand

During the ED I was sitting on the threes with another officer, who had many years in the job, when one of the officers from the fours came down and informed us that someone had 'fucking crapped in his cup'. It turned out that the officer had just made himself a brew when an inmate, who had just returned from attending his mother's funeral, asked to be banged up. The officer was happy to oblige, but on returning to his seat at the other end of the landing, he couldn't help noticing that the mug once brimming with steaming, freshly made tea was now brimming with a steaming, freshly laid turd. You had to admire the skill in being able to crap on demand, but it was another valuable lesson: never leave anything unattended.

Breakfast

I was on the hotplate again today, this time for breakfast duty, where I learnt that there was one thing even more dangerous than the chips to serve. Milk. The milk always arrived in an urn and never in a million years did it contain enough milk for the 132 inmates – not to mention the screws, who often and unofficially topped up the vitally important staff tea room milk jug. So the urn was always topped up on the QT with a couple jugs of water.

The slightly diluted milk was served using two ladles. One small ladle was for tea and coffee, and one large ladle was for the cereal and porridge. Simple enough, you might think. Unfortunately, most inmates are allergic to the mornings. Very few actually arrive for breakfast on time. Some never do and some are fashionably late. Often, those inmates at the top of the pecking order simply can't be arsed to walk down a few flights of stairs to get breakfast, so they will send a gofer down to collect their milk, although the prison rules officially stated that it was 'one man, one meal'. No one, but no one, was allowed to collect another man's anything. But it was a common Spanish practice for inmates to collect meals for someone else.

The problem, of course, was that Smith could collect his own tea milk but doesn't want his cereal milk, whereas Jones would pick up his own cereal milk and Smith's, Brown is collecting no milk for himself but will collect the two Conner brothers' cereal milk and the older brother's tea milk. Wilson will collect the younger Conner's milk and his own tea milk, but could I give Frenchie his cereal milk? By which time my head was about to explode, and I turned religious and started praying that I didn't run out of fucking milk. Or worse, that someone didn't come down and say, 'I want my milk', when I knew I had given it to someone else but couldn't remember who and, even if I did, I wouldn't say because the recipient would be in for a slapping and I'd not only be known as a bottleless grass, but also I'd end up with a shedload of paperwork.

At this point, my hands were shaking so much with the stress of it all that the once simple act of pouring a ladleful of milk into a cup or bowl became fraught with potential problems. If I spilled it, I'd be sworn at, and no doubt threatened by both my colleagues and the inmates, who by now would all have realised how useless I was. And God forbid I actually spilled it on an inmate, as I'd be wearing the fucking urn. It really was a no-win situation. I never thought I'd feel nostalgic for the good old days on chips.

Prison education

Another lesson learnt the hard way: when escorting an inmate from one area of the prison to another, keep the inmate positioned between yourself and the wing.

Today, I escorted an inmate from the Seg unit to reception. Only after collecting him and radioing the control room did I realise that this inmate had only a short time ago threatened a SO with a pair of scissors. He held them close to his eye and informed him in no uncertain terms that he 'would lose the fucking thing if he didn't get his milk' (apparently, they were one milk short – I told you serving milk was dangerous). This threat was far from idle, as he was a dangerous con with a history of assaults on both staff and other inmates. The scissors were gently pressed against the SO's lower eye lid, leaving a nasty mark. This inmate was only a little fella, small in stature and quiet. And by quiet, I mean he refused to talk to or acknowledge me or any other member of staff. He hated screws.

It was fortunate for me that the Seg staff were acutely aware of this particular inmate's history and the fact that

I was fairly new. They knew it wasn't wise to move this particular individual on my own, so as we left the Seg unit, they phoned the control room and made sure that I had camera coverage all the way down. And as we walked through the exercise yard, various projectiles came flying from the numerous cell windows on each of the landings: batteries, shit-parcels, glass, containers. Plenty of verbal threats and abuse, too. I was basically under attack.

The inmate, who was walking slightly ahead of me, smirked. I, on the other hand, had no choice but to try to look calm while surreptitiously trying to speed up. He was having none of it. He wasn't the target and he knew it, and he made sure he enjoyed his leisurely stroll down to reception. The attack was over within a matter of seconds and I had escaped without getting hit but had learnt a valuable lesson: always keep the inmate between me and the wing. It was also an insight into the amount of respect the dangerous inmate had from fellow inmates, and how quickly a group of inmates can rally round and work together as a cohesive team, a team with just one aim (no pun intended): to fuck about an officer.

Fourteen years later, this inmate returned to HMP Parkhurst and was in the Seg unit again. While I was doing my roll check, I opened the observation flap and a voice from inside said, 'Evening, Mr Berridge. See you're still here.' It was him. I had only ever had that single ten-minute encounter with him, during which he never spoke or acknowledged me. But he remembered me all those years later. It was, I have to say, a little unnerving.

A shit job

I was on detail for yards party this morning, which is the yard cleaning and litter-picking party. I was down for quite literally a shit job, supervising the shit-parcel collector, which, rather bizarrely, is one of the better jobs an inmate can have. It is lucrative for them and certainly adds a new twist to the old saying 'where there's muck there's brass'. Shit-parcels are exactly as they sound: parcels of shit that have been thrown out of cell windows.

Though shit-parcels are less prevalent these days, as all cells are now obliged by law to have internal sanitation, at the time, Parkhurst was in the process of being brought up to date with toilets in the cells. Prior to this, inmates were issued with the ubiquitous slop bucket. Despite the prison service's rather lavish spending, which saw them generously splashing out on a purpose-built odour-proof lid for the bucket, the ungrateful inmate would prefer, for whatever reason, to throw his crap out of the window. However, this was never going to be easy, as each window was too small. So the ever-resourceful inmate would crap onto a newspaper page, place it into a sock, old T shirt or any other item to hand and then, with the skill and dexterity of a seasoned origami master, fold the resulting mess into a handy-sized parcel that could fit through the window's small gap.

With anywhere between sixty to eighty shit-parcels a day being lobbed out of the various windows, business was booming. The shit-parcel collector was paid a bonus for each biohazard he collected and was never short of work, while the rats, pigeons and cockroaches were never short of a tasty meal. The collector's job was the highest paid but the most unpleasant, especially in the summer, when the all-pervading stench wafted around the prison.

Big boys do cry

Standing at 6 foot 6 and built like a brick shithouse, Winnie was the sort of physically imposing but none-too-bright inmate who could lift a ton but would have trouble spelling it. He was hired muscle, a thug and wing enforcer. No one messed with or argued with Winnie.

So I was greeted with something of a surprise tonight when I was doing the end-of-shift roll check – when we check and count the inmates in their cells – and I saw Winnie sitting on the cell floor, crying a deep, internal cry so genuine and uncontrolled that he actually looked like a small and very upset child – a child who needed his mum. The 'normal', human thing would be to ask what was wrong, but in prison this human response would be wrong on so many levels. His macho pride would mean he would have to tell me to fuck off, for starters. If I asked him why he was crying, his neighbours would hear and word would spread around the prison like wildfire. And, as harsh as this might sound, it really wasn't any concern of mine. He was alive and in his cell, and that was all that really mattered to me.

This was by no means an isolated incident among inmates. One thing that had genuinely surprised me in the job was just how many so-called hardmen actually cry. Tough guys who can beat the shit out of anyone and aren't frightened of anything actually crying behind closed doors, and yet as soon as the cell door is opened he, like a stage actor, slips into character, wearing his hardman persona and strutting his way down the wing.

Likewise the so-called straight, homo-hating alpha males who are happy to indulge in a little recreational anal sex, or the odd blow job or two. Though sex between inmates was strictly against prison rules, the confusing thing was that the healthcare department supplied the inmates with condoms – condoms that the prison service didn't officially allow them to use!

Collapsible furniture

Last night, an inmate managed to throw his whole cell out of the window. All the furniture and fittings were broken up into bite-size manageable chunks: sink, toilet, light fittings, clothing, bed plus bedding – the lot. When staff finally entered his cell, he was standing stark bollock naked inside what was little more than an empty concrete box. Even bits of the lino-style floor covering was now out on the yard. An impressive display of professional vandalism.

Talking the talk

Another officer escorting the yards party around the prison grounds demonstrated the folly of not being mindful of where you position yourself with the prisoners. This particular officer loved to talk and he talked for the sake of talking but, like most people who talk too much, he rarely had anything interesting to say. This particular day he was in full flow, in among a group of inmates who were no doubt enthralled by the verbal garbage he was spewing. Another three inmates were a short distance behind, one of whom was pulling the large wooden trolley half-full of recently collected bin bags.

In the middle of this officer's verbal barrage, his radio suddenly sprang to life: the control room informed him that his trolley was on fire. An inmate had thrown a flaming projectile out of a cell window, which had landed in the trolley and ignited the contents. The pyrotechnic display was impressive and only extinguished by staff from B wing running out with a fire extinguisher to douse the flames. The escorting officer should have been behind the inmates, observing, rather than in the middle of them talking his usual bollocks.

Blue light

Being blue lighted basically means being taken out to an outside hospital by ambulance. Today, a blue-lighted inmate was suffering from what the paramedics said was 'severe rectal trauma'. The hospital screws who initially examined him had decided that he needed to go out as he was bleeding and in serious pain. Years of catastrophic anal intrusion had caused major damage, damage that couldn't fixed in the prison hospital.

This inmate had used his bottom for many things, including the smuggling of illicit items, concealing contra-band, and for sexual pleasure and debt clearing. The frequency with which his poor old bottom had been fucked about had finally taken its toll and it was no longer fit for the purpose for which it was originally intended.

My first night shift

Tonight was the first of my first set of nights, which was seven consecutive nights, before I had a week off. I was on the Seg unit, the block, of all places. Nights in the Seg unit were, I was reliably informed, a 'fucking mare' – and even more so for a NEPO.

Approaching the wings on my way to the block, I noticed half a dozen lines being swung from one cell window to the next. They were improvised fishing lines, allowing everything from tobacco to drugs, from weapons to cassettes,★ and instructions being passed around the wing from window to window. Inmates were shouting, but it was difficult to make out specifics in all the noise beyond snatched fragments like, 'You listening?', 'There's a fucking kanga' (kangaroo equals screw), 'It's stuck', and 'He's just come down the chokey'.

I was given a five-minute induction on the basics (it had to be quick – the PO clearly wanted to get off home) and shown how the night-time 'pegging' system worked. This 'pegging' was required every half an hour, and was done by going onto either the north or south end of a particular landing and inserting a small key and turning it, which registered your location at that particular time (it was really designed to make sure you were still awake). Instructions and the location of the next 'peg' were clearly written on the pegging sheet to do half an hour later, so you might do the fours south and then half an hour later you might do ones north and so it went on. I was told that a NEPO the week before did *every* peg every half an hour, so he would have been pegging the fours, threes, twos and ones – and not necessarily in that order – every half an hour. I was politely asked not to repeat that behaviour if I didn't want an almighty bollocking in the morning.

★ Today it would be CDs, games or DVDs.

I asked why the fire hose was out. Apparently I would need it, and it was quicker to have it out and ready. The day staff had just finished damping down the outside of the cells, making sure everything was wet, because the inmates would throw rubbish out of the windows and attempt to set it alight.

Once the day staff left, I was on my own. I had just started to make myself a brew, when a cell bell went off and the fun began. The inconsiderate inmates wouldn't even let me have a cuppa in peace. I had been told that it was best to stamp your authority early on; once they realised you were a no-nonsense screw, they would wind their necks in. But if they thought you were a pushover, you'd be busy all night and all fucking week.

The first couple of cell bells were, I'm sure, just a test run, checking out who the new 'night clocky' was. I arrived at the first to be asked: 'Guv, can you pass this paper?' As I've said, 'passing' anything is a great big no-no. You don't pass things on a normal wing at night, let alone the Seg unit. It's wrong on so many levels. Plus, you don't have keys to open a cell door for that very reason – and the whole place has camera coverage, so you are constantly monitored.

Fortunately, I had been well briefed and the simple instruction was an unequivocal 'no passing'. Not that it stopped the cell bells, of course.

'Guv, can you get the ciggie papers from the cell next door?'

'Guv, have you got a newspaper I can read?'

'Guv, can you pass an envelope and some writing paper?'

'Guv, can you get me some hot water?'

'Guv, can you pass me a plaster?'

'Guv, can I have a khazi roll?'

On and on it went. And up and down the stairs I went. But the answer was always the same. I said no, and then a bit more no. To the normal person – anyone with a simple grasp of the Queen's English, really – no means no. It won't happen. I won't pass. Your request has been denied. But the inmates seemed to have translated it differently, as their response was that they would go to my house, molest my wife, kick my dog and pinch my car. Doors were kicked. My sexuality was questioned repeatedly. My life was threatened. Inmates, I decided, really don't like the word 'no'.

Once I had finished doing the roll check, I phoned it in to the control room and told them about the numerous requests. They laughed and told me of an officer a few months ago who was actually making the inmates toast. He made the toast in the staff kitchen area and then sent it up on a line to the inmates, which had all been filmed.

Unfortunately for me, the inmates' tirade carried on, but I had been told that if I could ride out the initial onslaught for the first night, the rest of the week would be quieter. Sure enough, by about 23.00 it had quietened down.

I was just in the process of sneaking around the threes, checking on the three ACCTs (Assessment, Care in Custody and Teamwork, a document that is regularly and at given intervals signed to say a suicidal inmate is alive) and pegging, when I heard the office phone ring. I made my way down, but as I reached the twos, the phone stopped and my radio sprang to life. The control room blurted out: 'Kilo 1.' (The Seg unit call sign.)

'Receiving, over,' I replied, only after turning the volume down.

They wanted me to contact 'E3' ASAP. E wing, threes landing, was in the hospital part of the prison and was

45

affectionately known to one and all as Fraggle Rock. A place where the seriously mentally ill inmates in need of constant medical supervision – or, as most of the screws called them, the headcases – were located.

I rang E3 and spoke to Del, a mildly excitable Scottish SO who had been there, done that and always led from the front. He 'led' you into a potentially dangerous situation as opposed to sending you into one, so he commanded a huge amount of respect among officers.

'Dave, I'm on my way to collect you,' he said. 'We've got one tooled up on E3.'

The problem was that I now had to pop next door onto A wing and ask the OSG to keep an eye on the Seg unit while we dealt with the emergency in the hospital. Understandably, he wasn't happy about it, as the Seg unit must be staffed by prison officers, not OSGs. And he was even less impressed when I told him I had three ACCTs. Along with his five, he now had a total of eight to keep an eye on – spread over two wings.

Del finally arrived and informed control that we were moving from the Seg unit to E3, as the last thing we wanted was some dog handler thinking we were inmates walking around the prison grounds and him letting Fido off the lead.

When we arrived on E3 we were told that Vincent, the inmate in question, had been in a funny mood all day and was now tooled up and unresponsive. He wasn't making threats or demands. He was, we were informed, just standing there holding an improvised bladed weapon.

I'd already had dealings with Vincent on D wing. Even with my limited medical knowledge, I knew that anyone who can eat a live budgerigar – yes, he actually popped a live budgie into his mouth, crunched, chewed, swallowed and was then quite literally spitting feathers – was likely in need of some psychological attention. He rarely spoke to staff and when he did it was usually a violent verbal volley of incoherent nonsense.

The immediate question was, why was he tooled up? Del, an OSG and I made our way to his cell, opened it up and spoke to him. Vincent was stocky and powerfully built. He just stood there staring into space. His improvised weapon was the ever-popular plastic toothbrush handle with a razor melted into the end.

Del tried again. Again, nothing. I stepped into his cell and, standing just front of him but just out of reach (just in case), I tried the friendly approach. 'Vincent, what's all this about?' I said. 'Give us the blade, mate.' He looked directly into my eyes, but it was like he didn't even see me.

Del and I were deciding how best to proceed, when the decision was made for us. With one swift motion, Vincent cut his own throat. The noise was like someone cutting through cardboard. The cut was deep, a single slice from just behind his left ear to the front near his Adam's apple. It opened up and then, after a couple of seconds, a torrent of blood followed. It didn't spurt or gush; it just flowed rapidly and pooled at his feet. It happened so quickly and yet at the same time felt like it was happening in slow motion. I just stood there for a split second, in shock.

Del snapped into action, grabbing a towel and calling the nurse. She arrived moments later and took the towel from Del then attempted to staunch the flow. Del then called for an ambulance. Vincent seemed to have snapped out of his trance-like state and was now sitting on his bed while the nurse desperately fought the flow of blood.

I immediately snapped out of my own shocked state and moved the now discarded weapon to one side. Vincent just looked at me and said, 'I've really done it now, Guv.' I couldn't disagree. 'Is it serious?'

The ambulance arrived, as did an extra member of staff in his very unofficial night-shift attire of jogging bottoms and polo shirt. And then Vincent, because of his unpredictable mental state, was finally taken to the outside hospital with four escorting members of staff.

I was just relieved he'd used the weapon on himself and not me or anyone else.*

Two nights later

The day staff had just finished putting out a cell fire when I arrived for my night shift. Once the admin was done, roll check completed and reported to the control room, and ACCTs checked and signed for, things seemed quieter than they had earlier in the week. It didn't last, of course.

A cell bell rang, and I just hoped it was a genuine emergency and not someone wanting me to switch their night light on or pass them a toilet roll. When I arrived at the cell I was greeted by the sight of an inmate who had carved himself up. He wasn't on an ACCT, but he was a prolific self-harmer. There was a lot of blood and his arms were in a bit of a state. However, I wasn't overly worried, as I knew that this particular inmate was an expert attention-seeker, adept at smearing the blood around to make it appear a lot worse than it actually was. The fact

---

* (Vincent survived the incident and later returned to the prison.)

that he was rolling a fag assured me that he was in no great distress.

I radioed it in, and Del and a hospital officer arrived to take a look at it. It was a little worse than my diagnosis and the hospital officer decided that two of the cuts were deep enough to require treatment in the outside hospital. This was, frankly, a royal pain in the arse, but at least this time the escort would only require two officers to go out with him, not the four that Vincent had needed.

Despite both arms being sliced and diced, he would still need to be handcuffed and as I was still the NEPO, that dubious honour fell to me. I had some claret on me, but thankfully the inmate preferred to turn to the hospital staff for small talk, where he was likely to get a bit more sympathy.

When the doctor checked the wounds at the hospital, he asked the inmate several questions – how did you do it, what with, why, how long ago? – and then fell into silence. He poked, probed and prodded at the arm and then asked the inmate, 'What's this? There seems to be something here.'

Without batting an eyelid, the inmate said, 'It's a pen.' He had not only cut himself, but had also shoved a biro pen up into his arm through the cut. There were other items, too: three prongs from a plastic fork and a paper clip. This wasn't going to be the quick stitching job we'd hoped for.

The other officer called the prison. We were lucky that it was still fairly early, just before 21.00, and thankfully, we were relieved about an hour later and returned to the prison. The inmate, however, required surgery.

Good night

This was the last night of my first set of night shifts. Thankfully, it was an uneventful shift until 04.20, when a cell bell sounded. That's a weird time, I thought. I'd learnt my lesson and hoped that it wasn't serious this time – I didn't fancy another trip outside and the prospect of getting home late. Fortunately, it was just some plum wanting to know the time.

CHAPTER 3

Prison Rules

1993

Attempted murder

Two Cypriot brothers were at the very top of the inmate hierarchy. They were convicted armed robbers, gangsters who ran a few allegedly legitimate businesses in London. Their money, power and status made them more or less untouchable, and little happened on the wing without their say-so. Half a dozen of their henchmen were on the wing, and any number of sycophantic followers, vulnerable people and those in their debt were at their beck and call. They had enough contacts, both inside and out, to make sure debts were paid, scores settled and people kept their lids on on the wing. Not for our benefit, of course. They asserted their influence to make sure their relatively cushy life inside remained that way.

So it came as something of a surprise today to find that a Turkish inmate by the name of Tokyo Joe was the victim of an attack because he was related by marriage to the two Cypriot brothers. We had just unlocked the wing and were making our way to the end of the threes, when Kev, a longer-serving and respected officer, and I both heard a peculiar noise – and a peculiar noise usually means trouble – from the fours.

Strangely, the wing was otherwise quiet. And that was usually an indication that the inmates were up to no good.

Just like kids, when they are making a noise it's annoying and irritating, but when they go quiet, something is probably wrong. We weren't wrong. Tokyo Joe was lying on the landing floor, face down in a pool of fast-flowing blood. I caught sight of two inmates disappearing into the association area, a recreation area of sorts, where inmates socialise and play pool during their association time.

We had a quick look at Tokyo Joe and it didn't need a medic to work out what had happened. He had been stabbed in the back numerous times – nine puncture wounds were apparent, and the blood was flowing fast and freely, making it difficult for us to stem the flow. I left Kev with Tokyo while I hit the alarm bell. I set off after the two inmates who had seemingly walked away from the crime scene into the association area, safe in the knowledge that backup was now on the way.

The two inmates weren't in any great hurry. They walked rather calmly – nonchalantly, even – into the small TV room and, before I got there, they came out, looked at me, smiled and walked on. This threw me. Had I misread the situation? Jumped to conclusions?

I returned to Kev and Tokyo just as one of the Cypriot brothers walked past and saw us tending to his injured relative. While we fought to stop the bleeding, the other staff arrived and, as usual, immediately started to bang up the wing. The medics arrived and, once the wing was banged up, Tokyo was carted off to the prison hospital. We told O1 what had happened and about the two inmates who had disappeared into the TV room. A dog handler was immediately sent to search outside the wing and an improvised weapon was found: a sharpened toilet brush, still fresh with traces of blood.

When we finally had a chance to make a much-needed brew, the SO came in and asked us to get cracking on the paperwork. 'Get it right, chaps,' he added. 'It might be used in a murder investigation.'

Borrowing

One thing an inmate should never do is borrow. It's against prison rules, which isn't always much of a deterrent to inmates, but it's against prison rules because it's dangerous. A gullible, desperate inmate is nothing more than fodder or prey, and the payback rates are extortionate.★

Many a time, an inmate would walk down the landing covered in blood and sporting a black eye or two. We all knew what had actually happened, but when challenged about the injuries and how they had occurred, the victim always turned out to be a victim not of an assault, but, would you believe it, his own clumsiness. Walking into a door not once, but several times. Prison doors are, it turns out, dangerous, causing more injuries to inmates than anything else.

The prison grapevine can be a useful tool, however, and we learnt that Tokyo had apparently run up debts of over a thousand pounds that he couldn't pay and even being married to the Cypriots' sister wasn't enough to save him.

We did get the paperwork right. Thankfully, it wouldn't be needed in a murder investigation. Tokyo survived,

---

★   At the time of writing, I was told by an inmate that the smoking ban had seen a half ounce of tobacco rise from £50 to £300.

but he wouldn't admit to being assaulted. Omertà, the code of silence, is one of the strongest rules in the prison environment, and few inmates are keen to turn grass and potentially earn themselves a death sentence. It did mean that we didn't have any proof to link the two inmates I'd seen leaving the scene to the crime. Nonetheless, Tokyo was to be transferred out of Parkhurst for his own protection.

Prison payments

There are many ways to pay for something in prison. Money isn't allowed in prison outside an inmate's 'spends' account, so IOUs or some discreet dealings over the phone would be required. An inmate can become 'employed' as a gofer. Running around, delivering or collecting stuff, or passing on messages. An inmate can be 'ordered' or 'employed' to hold something illicit. This is fraught with danger, as should the item be discovered, nicked or lost, it's down to the inmate holding the item. He would be in a world of shit unless he could get the thing recovered, whether through stealing or buying it back. Either way, the onus is on him. You can take someone out – beat them up or kill them – you can trade sexual favours or, if you have a particular talent – like drawing, painting, tattooing, hair cutting – you can trade these. I've seen methadone that has been swallowed and then regurgitated and sold on. And of course no end of 'plugged' things (which means they are carried in up the bum) like drugs, blades or messages, mobile phones, which are then removed and sold on. Anything can be traded and anything is for sale at the right price.

The day the wing went up

We nearly lost the wing today. The inmates, for whatever reason, decided that they weren't going to be banged up, so started smashing things, shouting threats and hurling anything that came to hand. An attempt of sorts was made to gain control and get as many away and behind their doors as we could, but it quickly became apparent that orders had been given by members at the top of the prisoner hierarchy that no one was to bang up. And should any inmate be stupid enough not to follow these instructions, the repercussions from other inmates would be far worse than anything that the prison service could invoke, and they all knew it.

In these situations, working out the what and why is a waste of time and effort. We usually deal with what we've got in front of us. It's not only a case of making sure you and your colleagues are safe and accounted for, but also the inmates and that any injuries are dealt with. Only then can you ask the what and the why. We were wary and apprehensive, though any sense of fear or worry usually only comes later when the adrenaline wears off and the reports are being written up.

Once the officers and governors realised that force alone wouldn't work, we were given instructions to withdraw from the wing, regroup, get the negotiators in and find out what the hell was going on.

At one end of the wing was the education department and at the other was the Seg unit. Once the wing had been cleared of staff, C & R teams were kitted up and placed in position in the education department. The Seg unit was closed off and more staff were deployed there to make it ready to receive up to half a dozen inmates. Dog handlers and officers formed a ring around the wing. The inmates might have had control of the wing, but it was secure and they were at least contained now.

The negotiators, who were specialist trained prison officers, attempted to open a dialogue with the inmates. After a couple of hours, the duty governor – who effectively does the hands-on running of the prison on behalf of the number 1 governor – arrived and started to try to reason with the pissed-off inmates. He tried to get them to see that eventually this would inevitably have to end one way or the other and things were going well: the smashing up had ceased, the shouting had stopped and a temporary calm had descended.

Suddenly, the gates at the Seg unit end of the wing opened and one of the more senior officers appeared. Jim had been in the job for years: he was as deaf as a post and as daft as a brush. He's the only person I have ever met who could be in two places at once: on a landing and in his own little world. He was now walking straight into danger with just his sandwich box and a copy of his preferred newspaper, *The Sun*, in hand. He looked around and proceeded to walk through the wing.

It was like a scene from a bad western film, the gunslinger walking into the bar and the whole place freezing. The silence was impressive – silence and a prison wing just don't go together. Sixty plus pairs of eyes followed Jim – the inmates were leaning over the railings on each of the four landings, just watching and waiting for something, anything to happen. The inmates talking to the governor fell silent and turned to watch Jim, then turned back to the governor and back to Jim, in total and absolute confusion. The PO who was in charge of the C & R team waved at Jim and beckoned him over. Jim waved back and sauntered his way over, oblivious to the dangerous situation that he was in.

It turned out that Jim didn't know it was a no-go area. Apparently, no one had told him. Being on Planet Jim, he hadn't heard the alarm, nor realised that staff had been redeployed and the wing evacuated. To his credit, though, he did wonder why it was so quiet when he walked through. The inmates, for their part, thought Jim was the hardest fucking screw ever to walk the landings, with balls the size of coconuts and more neck than a giraffe.

Jim was quietly ushered out of harm's way so that negotiations could continue and after a couple of hours, a sort of order was restored. Half a dozen inmates were taken to the block, prior to being transferred out, and a controlled unlock was put in place while a clear-up operation began. Jim, however, the meanest, most clueless gunslinger in the west, would take a long time to live this down.

Who's a pretty boy, then?

As a thank you for our efforts to restore order to the prison, we were treated to a free meal in the staff mess, which only employed civilians to serve and cook for the staff. With the type of inmates we had at Parkhurst, let's just say you wouldn't want to have your food prepared by or even in the same room as someone who would take great delight in adding their own special flavourings.

At teatime, half a dozen of us made our way to the mess, where I was looking forward to a well-earned cheeseburger, which would no doubt taste so much better knowing that the governor was paying for it. The burger duly arrived, but it just didn't look right. Now, I'm no gastronome, but something was definitely wrong and on closer inspection, I realised that the sesame seeds on the bun were missing. The odd one or two were there, as were the indentations where they had once been, but the seeds were not.

I asked the bloke who had bought the thing over to the table what had happened to the seeds. He explained that the cook scrapes them off and takes them home for his parrot.

Paying respects

For most of us, a funeral is a solemn occasion. It's a time for reflection, an opportunity to say our final goodbyes. For convicted career criminals, however, a funeral is often just another opportunity to be exploited.

Prisoners are entitled to ask to attend the funeral of a loved one. The prison would only grant the visit reluctantly and only for immediate family. Distant relatives or friends wouldn't get a look-in. There are plenty of hoops to jump through, with lots of paperwork and checks on an inmate's history and behaviour. And, just as when they have to attend an outside hospital, they are under strict supervision from prison staff. In reality, this means staff being away from the prison, where they're needed. Funeral escorts are, frankly, a pain, especially when they involve a respected member of the criminal fraternity.

An officer called Rick Scott – a NEPO, in actual fact – was off work on long-term sick thanks to an incident on a funeral escort at the hands of an inmate on my wing. The funeral had been for this inmate's brother, whose entire family were part of the fabric of organised crime in the London area. An SO, Rick and another officer, and a driver provided the escort for the funeral in London.

Once all the paperwork was done, the procedure was for the inmate to be searched and then cuffed to an officer. The inmate would remain cuffed throughout the escort. An inmate would never be uncuffed on an escort unless he was in hospital for a procedure, and even then he would have to pose no escape risk (such as being sedated). Rick was not long out of the prison service training college and, as always, the shit job goes to the NEPO. He was hand-cuffed to this inmate in the back of a sweaty van all the way to London, which in itself was bad enough, but it was made all the worse by the fact that this particular inmate really hated screws. He was a wretched recidivist who was happy to use violence, threats and intimidation. And then the funeral itself was fraught with potential problems. His brother had been higher up in the criminal hierarchy and the rest of the family had the potential to be problematic. Add drink, friends and criminal colleagues into the mix, and I think you get the picture.

The drive to London was strained, as these things often are, full of awkward silences sporadically interjected with meaningless, superficially polite small talk. Only when they got into London did the mood of the inmate seem to lighten. He became more animated the nearer they got to the cemetery, pointing out various scenes of his past misdeeds along the route.

Then he decided he needed to pee. The SO informed him that they were only twenty minutes away from the cemetery but that the police station was closer, so they could take him there (which is normal practice). The inmate pointed out that his mum's house was just round the corner, barely 200 yards away. The SO stood firm and said they'd use the police station. The inmate who was 'bursting' then said he could wait twenty minutes till they got there, as it would 'take time and be a pain to get to the cop shop'. The driver carried on and made his way to the cemetery.

Once the van was parked up, the closeting chain, which is a length of lightweight chain that affords the inmate a degree of privacy for things like medical examinations and going to the toilet, was put on. Everyone got out and left the driver with the vehicle. Geezers in sharp suits made their way over. There were welcome hugs, handshakes and head nods. The place was packed with archetypal villains and their molls. A couple of 'uncles' asked if the cuffs could be removed during the ceremony, but they were told firmly and politely that he would have to remain cuffed throughout the service.

With the burial due to take place in about ten minutes, the three prison staff plus inmate, to whom Rick was still attached, made their way over to the WC. A quick check was conducted to make sure the cubicle was empty and that there was no other way out, such as a window, before the inmate was free to spend a penny, with Rick in close attendance.

The other two officers engaged in a bit of people watching – or 'eyeing up the talent', as was made clear later – when, quick as a flash, the closeting chain was wrapped around Rick's neck. The inmate pushed him forwards and up against the wall. The two other screws turned just in time to see the inmate raise a knife to Rick and say, 'Get these fucking cuffs off or he dies!'

The SO attempted to talk to the inmate while the officer with the cuff keys legged it towards the now vacant cubicle, slammed the door shut behind him and locked it (to keep the keys safe, he'd claim later). Rick, in the meantime, gathered his thoughts enough to elbow his assailant, which unfortunately didn't have the desired effect: it simply annoyed him enough to use the knife. He stabbed Rick, prompting an almighty life-or-death struggle between the conjoined pair – and the SO ran off (to get help, he'd later say).

When the SO returned, Rick was slumped in the corner, covered in claret, and the SO attempted to get the inmate away from him. A couple of police officers, who were also at the funeral, ostensibly to observe the criminal gathering, suddenly appeared and wrestled the inmate away. They called for backup and an ambulance. The officer locked in the toilet with the cuff keys could be heard saying, 'Rick, what's happening? Is he still there?'

Backup arrived just in time, as some of the family members started to arrive at the scene, having been alerted by the sight of the two police officers running to Rick's aid.

The inmate was eventually – and unceremoniously – dumped in the back of the van to a chorus of abuse and threats from his family and friends, all while the rather forlorn-looking vicar gamely tried to keep things going. The officer who'd locked himself in the toilet was telling anyone who would listen that he'd had to keep the cuff keys safe.

The paramedics arrived and got to work on Rick. He had several slash marks, including one to the throat, and two stab wounds, which would have been more but for the fact that his uniform trouser belt took a couple of stabs from the blade and in all probability saved him from far worse injuries. He was loaded into the ambulance and taken to hospital.

It transpired that this was a pre-planned escape attempt. Plan A was thwarted when the SO wouldn't let the inmate use the toilet at his mum's house, where a weapon was awaiting him. Plan B was for the weapon to be hidden in the cemetery's toilet. Plan B was a close-run thing.

The officer who locked himself in the cubicle spent the rest of his short service trying to justify his actions (or lack of) to anyone who would listen, and the SO said that he ran off to summon help. No matter what the reason, Rick was lucky to be alive. Rick, to his credit, eventually returned to work after twenty-five months off and had a long career in the service.

The jockey club

We had another full staff briefing this morning. The security department had got a whisper that there was to be an attempted break-in. The word was that a lorry or digger would be used to breach the wall during the exercise period. We were to be extra vigilant and were reassured that the necessary steps had been taken, with the police being made aware of the potential threat and the dog handlers strategically located around the exterior of the prison wall.

After the meeting we made our way back to the wing and proceeded to unlock. Just as we had finished, Tommy Wisbey, one of the Great Train Robbers, who was now doing time for cocaine dealing, came down the landing stairs. Looking for all the world like Noël Coward, who played the criminal character Mr Bridger in the film *The Italian Job*, he stated in his best Cockney gangster voice, 'You cunts 'ave more meetings than the fucking jockey club!'

CHAPTER 4

Terror and Notoriety

In June 1993, as part of the ongoing mass renovation of the Victorian prison to bring it up to date and in line with standards of the late twentieth century, Parkhurst's B and M wings were closed for refurbishment, with the inmates moved en masse to the newly refurbished A and D wings. I was, along with other B-wing staff, moved to D wing, with the bulk of staff on M wing moving to A wing.

1994

The IRA

First thing this morning an inmate was called to see the governor. This particular inmate was Northern Irish, violent and dangerous. He hated the English, hated authority and hated females. Now, given that this governor – one of the better ones, as it happened: understanding, fair and respected among the officers and inmates – was English, female and, to top it off, heavily pregnant, not to mention that the news she was about to impart wasn't good, we had a recipe for disaster.

She had asked the wing PO to be in the office with her when she delivered the bad news. This PO was neither brave nor dynamic – his nickname was Bottleless Bob – but he understood that this inmate had a serious propensity for violence and asked three of us – the other two were longer-serving officers – to stand outside the office 'just in case it kicked off'. And kick off it did.

The inmate came storming out of the office, slamming the door open and throwing a chair across the ones landing. He then ripped his shirt off, looked towards the fours landing and shouted, in his thick Northern Irish accent, 'Are there any Irish men? This Irish man needs help!'

Within a matter of seconds, his distress call was answered by a few inmates, including some members of the IRA, who were now descending the stairs. Satisfied with the response, he then looked at the three of us and said, 'You're a bunch of fucking inbred cunts!'. Then he picked up an iron, which was on the ironing board outside the office, and threw it at us. We automatically took evasive action and hit the alarm. Fortunately for us, the iron, though hot, was still plugged in, so it didn't go far. The ironing board was next.

My heartbeat was working overtime. My mind was racing, desperately trying to process too many things: the inmates descending the stairs, the immediate threat in front of me, the alarm bells, shouts, threats and crashing furniture. Backup arrived, the heavily pregnant governor was escorted out of the wing and officers from all over the prison started to appear.

Now, we could get to work on restoring some sort of order, but there was a problem. The Irish couldn't and wouldn't be seen to back down, but then the two Cypriot gangster brothers seemed to take the initiative. They spoke to a couple of the IRA, who then disappeared. Staff were still arriving, but there was a definite stand-off: the inmates wouldn't move, certainly wouldn't bang up. If we decided to use physical force it would get messy very quickly and could have resulted in a riot.

Then who should make an appearance but Bottleless Bob. His coat on, sandwich box and folder under his arm, he explained that because he had worked through his lunch break, he was now knocking off early.

The IRA contingent finally reappeared, spoke to the pissed-off inmate and then one of them gave a gentle nod of the head to O1. They returned to their landing and banged up, and this was our cue to bang up the rest of the wing. I can't say that we regained control of the wing, but I can say with absolute certainty that we were given the wing back. It was a close-run thing.

The IRA were subtly dangerous. They saw themselves as a military unit, organising, watching and monitoring, always testing and probing for weak spots, gleaning and collecting all and any information, so when a problem or situation arose within the prison it could be exploited.

So with IRA members like Jimmy Canning – the IRA quartermaster whom the judge said was both 'dangerous and dedicated' before sentencing him to thirty years – and Sean Kinsella, a man who was part of a killer squad so deadly that they were found guilty of no less than fifty-five charges of attempted murder, conspiracy to murder and cause explosions – start getting involved and getting busy, you take it seriously. You switch on.

Fortunately, not all IRA members were housed in the same wing; some were housed in the SSU. Patrick Magee and Peter Sherry were both jailed for their part in the notorious 1984 Brighton bombing, when the IRA tried and very nearly succeeded in killing Prime Minister Margaret Thatcher and her Cabinet. Also housed in the SSU was Gilbert McNamee, a man who was dubbed an IRA 'master bomb maker' and was consequently sentenced to twenty-five years.* The IRA were extremely serious and exceptionally dangerous, and when you combine firearms and explosives with desperate and dangerous inmates, you will always have the perfect recipe for disaster.

We knew it had been bloody close to a pitched battle, which would have resulted in injuries to both officers and inmates, not to mention damage to the wing and another shedload of paperwork. The severity of the situation was confirmed when the number one governor came onto the wing. He listened intently as staff briefed him on what had actually happened, how it was resolved and the current location of the main instigator. Then, being the observant type, he noticed that on a few of the staff's personal lockers were posters and some harmless jokey banter – about each other's football teams and the like. The wing PO was told in no uncertain terms that they were to be removed and should any reappear, disciplinary action would be taken.

Teatime

Serving tea was the usual controlled chaos today. We had just about finished serving the sixty-plus cons, when an argument started. One of the newer inmates had for some reason decided to flex his muscles. Unfortunately for him, he picked on a lunatic. A.L. was a nasty piece of work, a Black Country pimp and a bully – a very dangerous individual. Before arriving at Parkhurst he had spent months

---

* His conviction would be overturned in 1998. Both Sherry and McNamee would later transfer to HMP Whitemoor's SSU, and formed part of a six-man team who made an audacious and very nearly successful escape attempt using two firearms and Semtex.

in a Seg unit and because of his propensity for violence, he arrived at our prison in a body belt. He was not to be messed with.

The two of them had a couple of choice words – about what, exactly, remains a mystery. A couple of angry glances were exchanged and then bish-bash-bosh! A.L. snatched a ladle from an officer's hand with lightning speed and grabbed his wannabe persecutor in a well-practised head-lock. He then rhythmically beat seven shades of shit out of his victim's head. Musically gifted he was not, but entertaining he most certainly was. This musical extravaganza was brought to an abrupt end when some party pooper hit the alarm bell.

Hostage situation

I was detailed to work in the Seg unit today – always an interesting shift. I was reading the handover book to catch up on the comings and goings of the wing. One of the comments said that an inmate had smashed up his cell, threatened to attack staff and self-harmed by cutting his arms. To top it all off, he'd then taken a hostage. Given that he was the soul occupier of the cell, that would have taken some doing, but you should never underestimate the resourcefulness of an inmate.

Necessity is the mother of invention. He couldn't really take himself hostage, so he improvised and took his penis hostage. He tied a ligature around it and refused to remove it until he was given a smoke. The swollen and discoloured penis looked to be, according to reports, in a pitiful state. But rules were rules and he wasn't going to get a smoke under these conditions.

What he did get was a hairy-arsed scab lifter informing him that one way or another the ligature would have to come off. To emphasise the point, he had a rather large pair of scissors in his hand as he explained that while he would do his utmost to remove the ligature without causing further damage to the poor, innocent penis, he could make no guarantees. Quitting smoking suddenly seemed like an attractive option to the inmate and he was more than willing to release his hostage. Disaster was averted, the poor old penis was saved from a rather sticky end.

The lowest of the low

Robert Peace was the Seg unit orderly and was very pro staff. His hulking physique and subtly menacing demeanour ensured that he could hold his own when dealing with the type of inmate housed in the Seg unit. What made him a bit of an oddity in Parkhurst was the fact that he was a sex offender. One of the truer aspects of prison life in popular culture? A rapist is considered the lowest of the low. Peace knew he was a marked man and he was sharp enough to know that he had a cushy, trusted job. Being pro staff ensured that his position and safety were, for him, as good as it was going to get.

Today, he was out and about on the ones, cleaning and mopping, when one of the officers came out the office and told him, 'There's one on the way', which meant someone from the wing was being escorted to the block for some reason or other. When the door linking the wing to the Seg unit opened, the PO told Peace, 'Just get behind the gate for a sec.' This was a metal-barred gate that separated the shower-cum-recess area from the Seg unit landing.

Peace duly went in and pulled the gate closed, just in time to hear the escorting officers arriving with the inmate, followed by the standard call of 'Seg unit, one on.' This call was to make sure no other inmate was out of their cell. You never take an inmate into the Seg if another inmate is out. Inmates in the Seg aren't to come into contact with other inmates; they are segregated for a reason.

The escorting officers and inmate descended the stairs. This inmate, Williams, hailed from the West Indies and was a particularly unpleasant piece of work, in for aggravated burglary of an elderly couple. Being the kind of person Williams was, he wasn't happy with just burgling a couple of pensioners. He tortured each of the victims in front of the other, breaking each of the husband's toes with a pair of pliers for nothing more than the fun of it.

When he caught sight of Peace locked safely behind the gate, he gave him a look and sucked his teeth at him. Peace, very slowly, pushed the gate open and, as Williams's jaw dropped in horror at the realisation that the gate wasn't locked, Peace delivered one punch with such speed and force that Williams hit the deck with an almighty thud. He was out cold.

Realising they would be in a whole world of shit if people up high found out about it, the officers dragged the unconscious Williams into the nearest empty cell and then put the kettle on. They rightly figured that Williams would never admit to being dropped by a nonce.

Dirty protests

There was a dirty protest today on the Seg unit. A dirty protest involves an unhappy inmate using his own excrement instead of the official channels to get his point across.

This kind of protest isn't as straightforward as it might sound, however. It can take many forms, the simplest of which would be to smear excrement around the cell. But inmates often up the ante by smearing both the cell and themselves in the stuff, while the sneakier, more calculated inmates might discreetly smear the stuff around, under mattresses, around door frames, in shoes, behind picture boards – anywhere that isn't immediately obvious.

Enterprising Seg unit cleaners could and often did make an absolute killing. Excrement and all matters faecal are big business in the Seg unit, and cleaners with a strong stomach and an entrepreneurial mindset knew that they would be able to cash in on a dirty protest. The cleaners and protesters can sometimes get their heads together and, as the cleaners get a generous bonus for cleaning the contaminated cell (this is regarded as a 'biohazard', so they get a bonus payment) on a daily basis, the cleaner might offer to split the bonus with the protester if he can continue 'shitting up'.

Today's dirty protestor was something else, though. He was a very intelligent, bookish type with a gift for calligraphy; he had the most beautiful handwriting. He could write prose that was a joy to read. The fact that he'd written it in shit today somewhat dimmed its beauty, but you couldn't argue with the fact that he'd quite literally turned the dirty protest into an art form.

Serial killer

The 'Fairy Liquidator' was a serial killer who had tortured and murdered five homosexual men during a four-month period. The press had dubbed him the 'Gay Slayer' and, shortly after arriving on A wing, he was keen to make an impression. He'd asked one of the big boys at the top of the wing hierarchy what would happen if he started to 'take out the faggots'.

This was never going to be a wise thing to say on a wing with at least 60 per cent of the population having indulged in some form of recreational homosexual activity. The whole wing would now be running scared, so the order had apparently been put out to get rid of him one way or the other. As soon as he left his cell today, someone set fire to it and burnt it out. It was a pretty clear warning and because of his high profile, it was acted upon immediately. He was removed from the wing and, as plans were already under way to transfer him out permanently, he was transferred ASAP.

Porridge

I was on the hotplate this morning, serving breakfast. Thankfully, I wasn't doing the milk. One of the first inmates in was Roger Andrews, a dangerous killer who hated staff, other inmates and the mornings even more than he hated himself. He had beaten a security guard to death during a Mickey Mouse burglary and in all the time he had been at Parkhurst, he had never spoken more than two words to staff.

Unfortunately for us, he was a powerlifter who had the dubious honour of being the first inmate to be put into the new Seg unit back in 1993. He wasn't in there long before he smashed up the brand-new cell. He had somehow managed to lift the bed off the floor, which, given that it was actually bolted down, was impressive. He had then bent the thing double before smashing the toilet and sink into tiny pieces.

There was no way he could be moved from that cell when he was so pumped up, so it was decided to let him calm down or tire himself out, whichever came first. But he kept banging the steel cell door so hard that it was actually moving, so two C & R teams were put on standby. He eventually wore himself out, much to everyone's relief, which is usually the case with powerlifters – they don't have the stamina and endurance, so burn out quickly.

This particular morning was porridge day, but it was only when he shoved his bowl over that we realised the porridge hadn't arrived at the hotplate. Before anyone could get to the kitchen and collect the forgotten porridge, Andrews went ballistic, kicking the hotplate and ranting and raving in his thick Scottish accent. Then he started throwing things. These things got progressively bigger, finishing with a fire extinguisher, which thankfully missed all of us. Everything had happened so quickly that no one had hit the alarm – but someone did now. Andrews was wrestled to the ground, the wing was banged up and he was taken to the block for the umpteenth time.

The day the bomb squad were called

I hadn't been on duty for more than an hour this afternoon, when the bomb squad were called. The IRA, along with an assortment of other terrorists and big-time gangsters, were always making threats to staff. Many of these threats were dismissed as being just claptrap, simply to intimidate. 'I know where you live', 'I know what car you drive' and the like. It required a lot of poker face and bluff to deal with this at times, and as several more experienced officers told me and I'd come to learn, after a while in the job an officer develops their own pocketful of answers to smartarse questions and threats.

Today, however, the threats became a reality. A dog handler and his canine companion were walking across the main staff car park, when something caught the handler's eye under a car. It appeared, at first glance, to be a small package about the size and shape of a shoe box. The dog also became extremely interested in whatever the suspicious item was, so the concerned dog handler quickly entered the prison rather than using his radio. He immediately went up to the control room and explained that there was a suspicious package beneath one of the cars.

The prison security department was immediately informed, the number one governor was contacted and the control room's camera operators went into overdrive, zooming in on the car concerned. They confirmed that there was indeed a suspicious-looking red-and-white package directly beneath the driver's seat, no doubt placed there to cause maximum damage.

The car park was immediately cordoned off and the police were called. The bomb squad were soon despatched. In the meantime, the control room staff checked the vehicle registrations and discovered that the car belonged to a member of staff, a PO no less. He was contacted and made aware of the fact that there was a suspicious device beneath his car. Thankfully, the control room staff record everything, so they started replaying the videos to see if they could catch the culprit. After trawling through the last couple of hours of footage, they caught their man red-handed. It was the PO himself. He'd placed the package beneath his own car.

It turned out that the PO had nipped down to the local KFC during his lunch break, sat in his car and eaten his meal. Rather than leaving the smelly empty box in his car or making the short walk to a rubbish bin, he opened the door and stuck the KFC box under the car before returning to work. The police weren't overly impressed and the bomb squad, who were now on their way over from the mainland, were called off.

Notoriety

Britain's Most Notorious Inmate is what the national press like to call him. And, to be fair, they have a point. Inmates feared him because of his unpredictability; staff were wary and cautious in their dealings with him. His reputation was based not on hearsay, but on deeds: he had a history of violence and hostage-taking. He had a big reputation and an ego to match.

This particular day, he was on the compound, which was basically a large exercise area with a football field, a couple of tennis courts and a sort of ad hoc garden area. As usual for a summer's weekend, the area was packed with nearly 150 of the country's most violent inmates, and having them all in one area always had the potential for trouble.

The compound had five small observation boxes strategically placed from which to view the whole area and cover any potential blind spots. An officer would man each box, ostensibly to monitor and deter any bad behaviour, and raise the alarm should anything untoward occur. The reality was that the officer had an hour or so to read the paper discreetly, do a crossword or sort out his annual leave. The more experienced officer would take a small flask of tea or coffee and spend a pleasant hour of peace and quiet away from the cacophonous wing. Unfortunately, the NEPOs only ever got this job in the winter, when it was pissing down with rain and freezing. If enough inmates wanted 'exercise', even if the weather was awful, then staff would have to go out. The IRA had a rota system that ensured enough prisoners went out, just to split the officers up and ensure we got cold, wet and miserable.*

Today, the weather was gorgeous – a bright and sunny afternoon. The POs were catching some rays, the inmates getting up to their usual discreet mischief – going quiet when walking past an officer if they were arranging business – and indiscreet mischief – making noise, talking rubbish and kicking the wooden observation box if the officer was reading or dozing, hoping to startle them.

One group of at least fifteen were discussing whatever it is that irritatingly noisy inmates discuss – and were noisy and irritating enough for the officer they walked past to almost spill his coffee. Once they'd passed his box, he continued with his crossword puzzle and cigarette rolling. It was only when he looked up while licking his cigarette paper that he noticed the group seemed to have walked over to and surrounded an inmate who was on the ground and struggling to get to his feet.

The by now annoyed officer, unlit fag in mouth, sauntered over and suddenly realised that Britain's Most Notorious Inmate was on the floor, covered in claret. The alarm was instantly raised and staff appeared within a couple of minutes, as did the medics. They immediately

---

* Nowadays, if it showers, looks overcast or is slightly chilly, exercise is cancelled due to 'inclement weather'.

attempted first aid on the bleeding inmate while the rest of us cleared the compound of prisoners.

Unfortunately, Britain's Most Notorious wanted nothing to do with any first aid. He slowly got to his feet, grabbed a handful of soil and rubbed it over and into his numerous and very obvious stab wounds. The medics tried in vain to convince him that he needed urgent treatment, but he refused, spitting out any and every profanity he could muster. His ego and his hardman reputation wouldn't allow anyone to treat him – that's what mere mortals did. He wouldn't be seen to be beaten or have any help from the screws.

He would, he said, make his own way back to his 'peter'.* So with a punctured body and bruised ego, he walked away, and how the blood poured. Escorted by officers and medics, and watched by dog handlers, he slowly and rather gingerly crossed the yard. The whole wing looked out of their cell windows at the bizarre scene unfolding below them as inmates strained to get a glimpse. The silence was palpable.

Eventually, through sheer willpower – fuelled, no doubt, by his huge ego and pride – Britain's Most Notorious Inmate hobbled and wobbled his way across the yard until he reached the wing, which was now being banged up. Once he got back to his cell, he collapsed in peace – and only then would he be taken to hospital.

Britain's Most Notorious Inmate was supposed to be dead. He had at least fifteen stab wounds and though there were no guarantees that he would survive, if he did there would be repercussions. Scores would be settled and the inmates, like us, knew it.

---

* Slang for cell.

Four days later

It transpired that a contract had been taken out on Britain's Most Notorious Inmate. No one knew why, but we did know that most of the other prisoners were terrified of his fearsome reputation and unpredictability. He had, however, survived the attack and we knew as well as the inmates that the shit would soon hit the fan when he returned to the wing. But according to the prison grapevine the matter was in hand – and the prison bigwigs were planning on shipping him out.

The Honey Monster

I was asked to man the gates (basically open and close the gates for a vehicle coming into the prison), as there was a vehicle coming in with the Honey Monster on board. Destination: the prison hospital, to recover from an operation at the local hospital. After he was located and secured, I stupidly asked one of the hospital officers why he was called the Honey Monster. He laughed and told me that it was because he'd just had an operation to remove a glass jar of honey from his arse. He'd stuck it up there the day before and found it wouldn't come out no matter how hard he – and some unfortunate prison staff – had tried.

1995

The infamous escape

On 3 January 1995, thankfully while I was on leave, three inmates on D wing, the wing I worked on, escaped from

HMP Parkhurst. This wasn't long after the escape from high-security HMP Whitemoor in Cambridgeshire, in 1994. The three Parkhurst inmates were able to make their own key (it was rumoured that one of them studied a member of staff's keys because he realised that when he was talking and emphasising something, he would hold his keys and point), make a ladder and even make an improvised replica gun. Apparently, one of the inmates was a qualified pilot and their plan was to steal a plane, but when that failed, they didn't appear to have a plan B. They were caught five days later, within a few miles of Parkhurst. While they had managed to escape from the prison, getting off the Isle of Wight had thankfully proved a hurdle too far for them.

Mistakes were made, of course, but concerns about the security of the prison had been raised long before. Staff raised concerns to the governor and the governor raised the issue with the Home Office with regard to the ongoing, extensive refurbishment in a high-security prison. Those concerns appeared to have been ignored.

Much has been written about the Parkhurst escape and numerous documentaries have been made. It was this escape that sealed my future in the prison services. Good, honest, hard-working staff were shat on, and arses were covered and arses promoted. Just take a look at the now infamous Jeremy Paxman–Michael Howard interview on Newsnight in 1997 to see how high the shit actually rose.

The one good thing, and probably the only good thing, about the escape was that the home office seemed to start throwing money at the place: money and resources that were once in such short supply were now seemingly unlimited, staff were sent to Parkhurst from a number of other prisons, the dog section had an increase in their numbers.

I remember one of the newly arrived officers asking me if I thought Parkhurst would lose its cat A status. I replied that I felt this was very unlikely. Why do you think that, he asked; it was a fairly easy and in my opinion a fairly obvious no brainer – we have the best perimeter, the Solent, they couldn't get off of the Island because of the Solent.

Shortly after this spending spree, HMP Parkhurst was taken out of the dispersal system after having its cat A status revoked!

The home office had spent many millions of tax payers' pounds, converting every single cell in four wings, A B, D and G wings, into super tough and super secure escape-proof cells all for nothing. They along with the national resources the SSU and C wing special unit and the dog section were now all surplus to requirement in a non dispersal prison.

Fire starter

Alarm bells from the hospital are usually the real deal. The hospital officers take great pride in managing some of the most damaged inmates in the system and they very rarely call for assistance. It's a pride thing; they like to keep things in-house. So when the alarm went off and all of our radios spewed out, *'Alarm bell, hospital – urgent assistance required!'* we took it extremely seriously.

We answered as a sea of white shirts descended on the hospital and went up to the E3 landing to deal with an inmate famous for being, frankly, a complete and utter nutter. When we reached his cell, we were treated to the somewhat surreal sight of a body wrapped head to foot in toilet paper, much like an Egyptian mummy. This wasn't fancy dress, though. He had somehow managed to get hold of a lighter and was now threatening to set himself on fire the moment anyone stepped into his cell. For good measure, he'd covered the floor in shredded newspaper, so that his cell was now nothing more than a tinder box ready to be ignited.

After twenty minutes spent trying to reason with the would-be pyromaniac, the by now pissed-off PO, famous for his short fuse, grabbed a cleaner's bucket, removed the mop and threw the stinking contents over the inmate. He was sodden, coughing and spluttering, and angry in the extreme, but very much alive.

Chatting with a couple of other officers over a brew later, we got a bit philosophical about it all. Saving the life of an inmate, no matter how despicable he is, is something that most prison officers will eventually do. It's part of our duty, a professional and moral obligation. Cutting someone down after an attempted hanging, breaking up a fight (often stepping into the fray and putting one's own safety to one side), pulling them out of a burning cell, removing an inmate from a particular wing or area, opening an ACCT or administering first aid – it's just what we do.

In the real world, saving a life is an act worthy of praise. There's a feeling of satisfaction, at giving someone a second chance; a job well done. Unfortunately, in prison, that life-saving act can often be met with a degree of derision. Saving the life of a child rapist, murderer or someone who has attacked a colleague doesn't give you the same feeling of satisfaction or well-being. It leaves a bittersweet taste. But we do it regardless.

Drinking and the job

There was an officers' club just across the road from the prison, a place for prison officers and their families to meet, unwind and socialise, and play darts, pool and cards. The club even had its own bowling green, which held regular tournaments. After a particularly bad shift staff would often nip in for a 'swift one' to unwind before heading home. The unfortunate thing was that there were a lot of bad shifts, which resulted in the club doing a roaring trade.

The drinking culture was huge and the expected macho norm. It started to become a problem, however, when an officer who was quiet, diligent and professional in the morning would pop over to the club at lunchtime for a swift one (or several) and return to the wing full of Dutch courage, often nasty, obnoxious and aggressive.

I was cuffed to a prisoner known for having a real attitude and hating screws. As was so often the case, he was a big guy, a brick shithouse built by steroids. Worse, he also had a personal hygiene problem and some pretty pungent bodily odours that I didn't want to spend inhaling any longer than I had to. Unfortunately, the officer attempting to apply the handcuffs had had a liquid lunch, and was now the proud owner of a short fuse, bad attitude and diminished coordination. He kept 'nipping' the inmate's wrists by mistake. He pinched the skin three or four times on the increasingly pissed-off inmate's wrists before the inmate realised that the officer had been drinking. He reeked of the stuff – the smell of alcohol on his breath was strong enough even to mask the inmate's BO.

The inmate got more and more agitated before he finally said to me, 'The twat's been drinking.' This put me in an awkward position. It was obvious to anyone he'd been drinking; I couldn't deny that. But I also couldn't admit it, so I did what I usually did in this kind of situation and bullshitted my way out of it. I told the inmate that he'd been to a party last night.

These days prison social clubs are thankfully a thing of the past, much like the drinking culture. Very rare is it that an officer turns up for work with a drink or several inside him. I'm sure there are the odd occasions, but it is virtually non-existent – in Parkhurst, at least.

As good as his word . . .

'Governors' Apps' was a daily occurrence, in which an inmate could request a meeting with a governor via an application form. It was then up to the governor to decide whether the request warranted a meeting or, as was usually the case, not. If it did, the governor would come onto the wing and see a particular inmate in the wing office.

Today, one of the governors came onto the wing to have a meeting with a rather volatile, intimidating inmate – one who had been sent to HMP Parkhurst with a horrendous record. As was the norm, an officer stood outside the office just in case things went pear-shaped, where the governor decided to use the word that all inmates hate, 'no', and things kicked off. After twenty minutes, the happy inmate emerged from the office wearing a grin that suggested he was very pleased indeed with the result of the meeting.

We fed the wing their lunch and banged up; however, shortly after unlock, the governor phoned the wing to tell us that, on reflection, his decision had been a little hasty.

We were to inform the inmate that the answer was going to have to be no.

Needless to say, it didn't end well. The inmate made threats to staff and then smashed his cell up, which resulted in a C & R team being deployed. The wing was banged up prior to the inmate being removed to the block, creating a domino effect, which resulted in the other inmates becoming royally pissed off. It's a shame the governor wasn't there to see it.

The scream I can still hear

Curry was a particularly nasty inmate. Quiet and self-assured to the point of arrogance, he was a loner who thought himself superior to his fellow inmates. This certainly didn't make him the most popular guy on D wing, and when some feelers were put out by a few of his fellow inmates to find out what he was in for, his popularity would plummet further still.

The prison grapevine is fantastically effective and it wasn't long before a background check on Curry returned the news that this inmate wasn't the usual run-of-the-mill armed robber, terrorist or murderer. No, it transpired that he was the lowest of the low: a rapist.* But even that label didn't do justice to the horrific details of his crime. He had actually raped his victim using two Dobermann Pinscher

---

* It was extremely unusual to have a sex offender on the wing, but he was one seriously dangerous inmate and couldn't be kept with other sex offenders. He had outstayed his welcome elsewhere and was consequently sent to Parkhurst in the forlorn hope that he would 'blend in' and survive.

dogs and the assault went on over a period of several hours. Once the inmates found this out, his fate was sealed.

A contract was put out. A contract payment in the prison can take many forms. It could be to pay off a debt or part of a debt. It could be to earn respect, for profit or indeed self-preservation. In its simplest terms, it's a 'quid pro quo' arrangement. 'You do me a favour and I'll do you a favour.' It's a verbal contract, of course, and could involve a debt being cleared by brewing and storing hooch, holding drugs, getting drugs or anything else smuggled in, potting (throwing faecal matter at) an officer – any number of things. Cash might be paid to a family member on the out, or payment might involve sex, information, tattoos – anything and everything has a value. Putting a contract on someone like Curry is a common occurrence and nothing might have been paid; it might be done for pleasure or brownie points.

Unfortunately for those in prison, life is cheap and somewhat precarious. A wrong look, wrong word, the slightest misunderstanding or rumour – whether it's based on fact or not is irrelevant – could potentially, and often does, result in payback. This payback takes many forms: a slight slapping, serious stabbing, a bloody beating, rape or murder, to name just a few. Or, in Curry's case, an attack using easy-to-hand ingredients.

Within a short space of time, the contract was fulfilled. During association, Curry was sitting watching the television in the small, dimly lit TV room, when two inmates calmly sauntered up behind him, pulled his head back by his hair and poured an entire jug of hot cooking fat mixed with sugar onto his face. Curry let out a blood-curdling cry that sent shivers down my spine. It was inhuman, like an animal in its death throes. I can honestly say that I have never heard screams like it in my life.* And I've heard a few.

The burns were, of course, severe. By the time we arrived, layers of his skin were peeling away and the usual remedy would be to use cold water to cool the burns. However, the weapon was chosen wisely: sugar had made the concoction sticky, while the fat ensured the water would be ineffectual (water and fat do not mix well). Hot cooking fat with sugar ensured that the concoction stuck to the burning flesh, which would slowly and painfully continue to burn. He immediately turned pink as large, blotchy bits of flesh fell away. The alarm was raised for the hospital staff, who removed him from the wing before he was transferred to a specialist burns unit. He lost an eye and very nearly his life.

---

* Nor have I heard anything like it since. It's an incident that still makes the hairs on the back of my neck stand up.

CHAPTER 5

Special Unit C Wing

I started on C-wing secure special psychiatric unit a few weeks ago. I volunteered for the job, as I wanted the experience of working with the most challenging inmates, and managed to get through the interview OK. This small wing housed sixteen of the most dangerous inmates in the country – inmates that even Broadmoor wouldn't take.

The criteria for Broadmoor was that an inmate must be curable, or at least be able to benefit from the care and treatment offered in such a secure hospital environment. But if they were beyond that, they were sent to C wing special unit.

Disruptive, violent and with a history of mental health problems – they had a litany of assaults on staff and other inmates to their name, and at least two of them had committed murder while inside. These inmates would traditionally have been kept in cat A conditions, a secure mental hospital, or the Seg unit, none of which were great solutions. So C wing had been set up as a way of treating the most challenging prisoners in the system. This unit was a national resource. If an inmate anywhere in the country met the criteria and had mental health issues so serious Broadmoor wouldn't take them, they would come here. It was staffed by a multidisciplinary team: resident psychiatrist, a couple of psychologists, probation officer, hospital officer, a couple of SOs, a PO and half a dozen officers – now including me, of course.

The pen is mightier than the sword

An officer was escorting a party of seven inmates from one of the wings down to reception, when one of the inmates asked the officer if he could borrow his pen. The officer duly obliged, whereupon the inmate said, 'Thanks, Guv,' and promptly stabbed another inmate three times, including once in the eye. Then he had the audacity to hand the pen back to the officer with a cheery, 'I needed to do that!'

Mango Daley

One of the newer governors has decided to make his mark. New, overly zealous governors seem to change things for no other reason than to say they've updated, improved, re-evaluated, altered, risk-assessed and come up with a brand-new bright idea. The latest brand-new bright idea was that staff weren't to bring rucksacks or bags of any description into the prison. So, officers being officers, we went to the stores and collected the old plastic slop buckets. So now the tea, coffee, lunch and gym kit we brought in was being carried around the prison in prison-issued slop buckets.*

I arrived for work this morning and an officer by the name of Mango Daley was walking across the car park, having just finished his night shift, carrying a wooden mop handle. When I arrived at the gate and collected my keys, I asked the gate officer what Mango was doing with a mop handle. 'He's taken one home every day so far,' he said. 'He's building a fence!'

---

* Needless to say, the order was soon withdrawn.

Mango got his unfortunate nickname because many years before, at another prison, he had left an officer to get badly assaulted rather than face the attacker. He was quickly moved from that prison and was consequently called Mango because he was green on the outside and yellow on the inside.

Mango was a kleptomaniac as well as a coward. He couldn't help himself. His light-fingered reputation preceded him, however, when he stole a whole box of black bin liners left tantalisingly on display. The staff had carefully sliced the bottoms of all 200 bags with a knife, leaving a boxful of bottomless bags as bait for a bottleless officer.

Visits

Punchy Pete was an enforcer and debt collector for London gangsters. At one time a useful amateur boxer, drugs and one too many punches to the head had left him ever so slightly brain damaged. His wife and six-year-old son were visiting, and his son by all accounts had been a bit of a handful, running around the visits hall shouting and generally being a problem child. Bill's wife told the kid to behave and then, *bam*! Punchy Pete punched his wife so hard he knocked off her seat and then yelled, 'No one, but no one shouts at my little Billy!'

The SO in charge thought he'd said, 'No one shouts at my little willy!' The alarm was raised, and we raced to the visits area in time to see Punchy Pete being wrestled to the ground and removed, all to a cacophonous and violent verbal volley from Mrs Punchy Pete. Ladylike the language was not. Some visitors clapped and cheered, while others took advantage of the melee for a quick grope or to pass something on. The visits area is under surveillance throughout family visits, so we checked the cameras to see exactly what had gone on and restored some kind of order.

Visits is one of the less popular jobs. While for the inmate it offers the opportunity to reconnect with the outside world and see loved ones, for a prison officer it can be a nightmare. Its *only* saving grace is that once the visits have finished, the visits officer is often surplus to requirements and can take a flyer (go home early). But that's the only good bit about it.

Many of the inmates' wives and partners despise us only slightly less than the police, as they see us as being the ones keeping their loved ones away from home. The inmates, of course, have tales of woe about the nasty screws who bully, beat and pick on them. They are hardly going to put a positive spin on a prison officer's lot. But the worst thing about visits is the children.

The kids of many of the criminal fraternity often grow up seeing authority figures like the police and prison officers as the enemy responsible for Daddy not being at home. So Mum sees a visit as an opportunity for a little payback. Kids already exhausted from getting up at the crack of dawn to travel to the prison are fuelled with chocolate and Coca-Cola, and it's a bit like throwing a hand grenade into the visits area. Hyperactive, loud, smelly and obnoxious little toerags under instruction to annoy the nasty screws play havoc. Sticky little fingers are smeared over anything and everything. Snot and God knows what else finds its way into places you wouldn't believe. Children coughing and picking their nose then wiping it wherever they like. Then running around in circles, making themselves dizzy – then one of them starts to feel nauseous and vomits all over the floor. Mum says sorry with a smile and removes the child, but leaves the vomit.

Give me a murderer, armed robber or terrorist any day over one of their children. At least you can reprimand a criminal. But taking a hyperactive seven-year-old covered in chocolate and vomit to task? No chance.

CHAPTER 6

A Wing and a Prayer: Beirut

One wing was known to all of us as Beirut and, as you might have inferred, it was a tough and demanding wing to work on. The inmates were officer-hating discipline problems. They would fuck about, fight and make life as unpleasant as possible, not only for the staff, but also for each other. The good thing was that the team of officers who worked there were a tight-knit group, professional and skilled. I loved it. I loved the challenge and in the four-and-a-half years I worked on it, there were stories of money changing hands between officers to avoid working on the wing. An officer would occasionally be detailed to work a morning, afternoon or ED and rather than work on the notoriously difficult A wing, they would pay someone cash to do the shift for them.

Many a time I heard that A wing had no-go areas. It transpired that these so-called no-go areas were like J.R.R. Tolkien's Middle-earth: an imaginary place. They were invented by staff who were, if we're being kind, somewhat reluctant to go into a particular area on the wing.

1996

Intelligence

Canteen day was always interesting. The inmates had a

budget to spend on things like tobacco,★ sweets and toiletries. They collected their weekly canteen from the hotplate, issued in transparent plastic bags. They checked to make sure everything was there and once they were happy it was all OK, they signed a receipt. The good thing about canteen day for the switched-on officer was that it was an opportunity to glean some intelligence on the comings and goings in the prison covertly. By standing on the landing and watching, you learnt to spot things like who is in debt. An inmate with three bags of canteen who goes into a cell and comes out with two, one or even no bags has probably used it to pay some or all of his debt off – or at least has paid the bully not to beat the shit out of him. A non-smoker who has just bought a load of tobacco, but on inspection has no tobacco in his possession, raises questions. The guy who usually goes to collect his canteen but doesn't do so this week leaves an officer to wonder why. A quick check of his 'spends account'† confirms he has enough money, so why doesn't he need his canteen this week? Is he suicidal, pissed off, planning to go to the block or frightened? Little things that go against the norm always raise concerns.

Sugar is another good example. In the real world sugar is just sugar; however, in prison sugar can be used for more than just a cup of tea. It's used in brewing hooch, as an additive for a scalding assault (as we've already seen) and some enterprising inmates even sprinkle sugar on the floor

---

★ Which is no longer allowed in prisons – at least officially.

† Which is like an individual bank account an inmate can withdraw from and spend on certain things within the prison, such as sweets, tea bags and shampoo.

as a crude but effective early warning system at night to hear a screw approaching.

When inmates who don't normally buy sugar start buying it and then hand it over, it always raises suspicion. Who has he given it to? And why? Why does that inmate need such a large amount of sugar?

Once canteen is over, the experienced officer has a wealth of intelligence gleaned from simply standing on the landing and watching.

These days, the knowledge that has been gathered and stored away in the officer's memory for later use would have to be papered up. Now, while I can see the value in sharing this information with the other officers – something we would do anyway in person – what it means in reality is an officer in an already understaffed prison would spend the next hour and a half glued to a computer screen, writing out reports in triplicate, instead of on the landing where he is of far greater use.

Blood is thicker than Ribena

Scary Mary was undoubtedly a character. Standing at only around 5 foot 4, he was as camp as Christmas and a bit of a drama queen. He lorded around the wing dressed in bespoke customised clothing: on him, shirts became blouses and jeans became shorts. Really tight shorts. So tight, in fact, that they displayed to all and sundry what can only be described as a male version of the camel toe. Mary's long, flowing, rapidly receding hair and hands that a navvy would be proud of (except for the coloured fingernails) cut quite a sight on the wing. Mary had been inside for years, and enjoyed making the new officers blush and squirm with embarrassment.

Mary was also a hard bastard, as anyone prepared to flaunt around in make-up and blouses on a wing full of really hard bastards had to be. And the 'scary' in his name was there for good reason: he was a cold-blooded killer, through and through.

Scary Mary and Crusher were an item. Crusher was bald, muscular and sported a rather nifty Mexican drop-handle moustache. He looked like a circus strongman. He loved Mary and Mary tolerated him. Today, there was an almighty commotion emanating from Crusher's cell. I raced to the cell with another officer – nicknamed Nappy Rash because it was the only excuse he hadn't used to call in sick. We got up the stairs to find Mary being escorted out of the cell by another inmate, and when we entered, we found Crusher crying and covered from head to toe in claret.

The alarm was raised and the process of banging up the wing began, which was easier than usual because the inmates would sooner be behind their doors than on the landing with a pissed-off Mary. The medics arrived and immediately realised that Crusher wasn't, as we had so hastily assumed, covered in blood from one of Mary's trademark stabbings, but rather it was blackcurrant juice. Mary had battered him with a plastic bottle of Ribena. He was still crying and explaining to anyone who would listen that he loved Mary, she was his wife – 'Guv, please don't split us up.' It was very touching Mills & Boon stuff.★

★ Many years later I heard they were still together, inseparable and still having the odd domestic.

The blizzard

I was on the threes today, when I heard a loud bang on the fours and was met with the surreal sight of what at first appeared to be mist rolling along the landing. It took a moment to realise what had actually happened: several fire extinguishers had been let off.

My immediate thought was that there was a fire. I raced up to unlock an inmate who had just been banged up, but for some reason my key didn't work. I couldn't insert the thing. As I went down the stairs, I noticed that the other officer had disappeared.*

The powder from the fire extinguishers was now settling down below. It looked like it was snowing, and everything and everyone was covered in a fine white powder. The alarm was raised and then from the ones came instructions to bang up the wing. It was only then that I realised why I hadn't been able to unlock the cell door on the fours. It wasn't an isolated case: every single cell lock had been 'pencilled', which meant a pencil or some other item had been pushed into the lock and snapped off, rendering the whole locking mechanism useless.

Backup arrived as other staff answered the alarm. But it was chaos. Staff and inmates alike were covered in white powder, making it difficult to distinguish one from the other, friend from foe. Breathing became a challenge. Alarm bells were ringing, staff were appearing from all over the

---

* I learnt many months later that this officer had done a runner, realising that the inmates had decided to take over the wing, and with discretion being the better part of valour, he'd decided to leave me to it.

place, and inmates were leaning over the railings, shouting obscenities, laughing, watching, studying us and no doubt counting us, weighing up the odds. Then the banging started. Kicking, hitting, smashing doors, walls, floors – anything that could be hit was hit. The noise was intense and the enclosed wing became an echo chamber, sounds reverberating off the walls. The cacophony was extreme and disorientating; I couldn't hear the officer next to me and we relied on hand signals.

The standard practice of immediately banging the wing up wasn't a viable option, so it was decided to evacuate and get those inmates we could onto the adjacent exercise yard. Those who couldn't or wouldn't were to be moved to the association area – containing two small kitchens, a pool room, TV room, toilet and a couple of small store-rooms – and then we would do a roll check. This was much easier said than done. The inmates had engineered this mass disruption, and were obviously pumped up and spoiling for a fight.

Another officer and I made our way to the association area, which was somewhat overcrowded, filled as it was with a couple of dozen testosterone-fuelled, angry inmates. This roll check was going to be a challenge. One wrong move, one wrong word, a wrong look . . . absolute caution was required. Now was most definitely not the time for heroics.

We cobbled together a plan of sorts: I took the left, my colleague the right, before meeting up and tallying our number of inmates. No chance. We both had no idea. The inmates had made sure we couldn't count by moving around, using verbal aggression and intimidation tactics – and the old favourite, shouting out random numbers. There was a loud bang. The pool table was on the move.

The super-tough Perspex windows were now being tested like never before. The smell of smoke and the shouts from inmates informed us that someone had set a storeroom on fire in this confined area.

The smoke quickly became dense. The inmates, now starting to feel a little panicked themselves, shouted, 'Open the fucking gates! Get us the fuck out of here!' They were right, we needed to get out, but releasing them into an already volatile wing would be like pouring petrol on the fire. We needed to know what the situation was before unlocking the gate.

I moved towards the barred gate, where a suitably hulking and pissed-off inmate was holding on to it. I tentatively approached and offered the most forceful, 'Excuse me,' I could manage. I was met with a very clear and very concise, 'Fuck off.'

Never one to give up – or perhaps just plain stupid – I tried again, only this time a few other choice words were added to my being told to 'fuck off'. He fixed me with a menacing glare, a glare I felt sure he had some practice at using – no doubt with some degree of success. I stepped back – hopefully just out of arm's reach – and thankfully I managed to catch the eye of an officer walking along the landing. I didn't have to say anything – the expression I was no doubt wearing must have told him that I thought I was about to die. He radioed down to the ones and then there was the heavenly sound of half a dozen screws running up to let us all out. Only then could we actually complete an accurate count of the inmates, which was twenty-seven; though in that small association area it had felt more like 127.

The wing was eventually evacuated and once they were accounted for, all the inmates were moved out onto the exercise yard. We finally got down to the serious business of firefighting, damping down small fires with fire hoses and any remaining extinguishers, and checking each of the small association rooms. Then the works department locksmiths came in and cleared all the locks.

Finally, the inmates were escorted in small groups back to their cells. Three cells were so badly damaged that they were out of use for now and four inmates were relocated to the Seg unit.

Man's best friend

One of the dog handlers arrived for work this morning. He pulled up in the staff car park, opened up the back of his van and realised that he had forgotten a vital component of his job: his dog. He set off home to retrieve his faithful − and no doubt bemused − hound. The resident cartoonist★ had a field day.

Food fight!

I was on an early shift today. The morning was, as per usual, chaotically busy and as we got ready to serve lunch, I was really looking forward to knocking off once we were done and the inmates banged up.

Nige was the cleaning officer for the day. A former soldier, Nige was one of those clean-shaven, immaculate individuals with the creases in his shirt and trousers just

---

★   This was an officer who had once worked as a graphic designer and now did cartoons of any funny moments or cock-ups. I believe most prisons have a cartoonist doing likewise.

so, his shoes always shined like black mirrors and never a short hair out of place. He worked in much the same way: fastidious, precise, punctual, which was, of course, bloody annoying for the rest of us mere mortals.

As Nige was holding the meal board, seemingly standing to attention while he read out each and every inmate's name and corresponding meal number, one of the inmates had the audacity to collapse. He hit the deck with an almighty thud, and then started shaking and convulsing. This particular inmate had a history of epilepsy and would have a fit two or three times a week. We were all aware of this and the only intervention we normally applied was to make sure he didn't hurt himself.

Nige, unperturbed, gave the inmate a withering glare, a glare that seemed to say, 'How dare you interrupt my hotplate.' Nige then continued reading off the names while he gently stepped over the fitting inmate.

Within seconds, pandemonium ensued. He was called a 'fucking cruel, heartless bastard' and much worse before things turned very nasty, very quickly. Food, plastic plates and bowls were all being thrown around. The alarm was raised and the cavalry arrived to rescue us from the war zone the hotplate had become. My lunchtime finish was now nothing more than a pipe dream and I was covered in three or four types of food, as were most of the rest of us. Nige, on the other hand, looked as he always did: bleedin' immaculate!

Keeping your mouth shut

I was on the twos today, talking to an inmate, when a cell bell went off. Unfortunately for me, the inmate I was talking to pointed out that it was the cell behind me. The occupier of this cell was a nuisance and a known self-harmer. He also spoke a very limited amount of English, or so he said. One thing you find in prison is that many of the non-English speaking inmates are actually capable of speaking perfectly good English, or at least understanding perfectly good English, when it suits them.

So, with a degree of trepidation, I looked through the observation panel and confirmed that my trepidation was well founded. It appeared that the idiot inmate had somehow sewn his own mouth shut. I shut the observation flap and rather than hit the alarm bell, went downstairs to get a coffee, then one of my colleagues joined me. I explained the situation before we both entered his cell and were able to confirm that he had indeed sewn his lips together using thin strips of wire. It looked a mess – an accomplished seamstress he was not.

We asked him why he had done it and he was under-standably even less communicative than normal. He mumbled, hummed and shook his head. We contacted the healthcare team and warned them what we were about to bring their way. They didn't believe us until we actually turned up. The nurses immediately noticed that his lips were swelling. He looked like a poor man's Pete Burns and the swelling was putting an enormous strain on the stitching, which looked like it could buckle at any moment. The inmate initially refused treatment, but they insisted, showing him what was happening in a mirror while they gently proceeded to snip away at the wire until he once again had lips that were capable of sinking ships.

I left them to it and returned to the wing, where I filled out a 'self-harm' form and wrote out the incident report, then opened an ACCT. I was now knee-deep in paperwork because of his attention-seeking stupidity, so I placed him on report for the destruction of prison property.*

Man's best friend (part II)

I'd barely had time to put the kettle on, when the alarm was raised for an 'officer down' on the compound (the exercise yard). We got there to find one of the dog handlers had collapsed, though no inmates were involved. However, when the medics tried to get near to the collapsed dog handler, the dog went ballistic. Still attached to the handler, the dog wouldn't let anyone near – it was snapping, yapping, barking, growling and warning everyone to keep away. The dog's intentions were good – he was protecting his handler – but the officer was in need of urgent medical attention, so another dog handler was called to deal with the dog before the medics could deal with the officer. It took over half an hour but fortunately, the dog handler was treated in time and made a full recovery.

The chopping board

Scary Mary, when not arguing with Crusher, worked in the kitchen and had done so for some time, where he was queen bee. Today, a new inmate started working there and upon arrival hung up his newly issued kitchen coat. The unfortunate thing for him was that he had chosen Queen Mary's peg. One of the wiser inmates collared the new inmate and told him of his mistake. The inmate, obviously

---

* The nicking, as expected, was later thrown out.

keen to stand his ground and show how hard he was, said, 'So fucking what? It's mine now and I ain't moving it. If the faggot's got a problem, he can see me.' At a little over 6 foot 4, built like a brick shithouse and with a history of armed robbery and violence, he was, it would be fair to say, an intimidating presence who thought he had good reason to stand his ground.

Mary, of course, had other ideas. Not for him a word in the new inmate's ear or even a threat. He simply walked over, picked up a knife and – unusually for a prison attack, in which a home-made shank is usually the weapon of choice – stabbed him repeatedly. His victim died within minutes from seven stab wounds. He never stood a chance.

This was the third inmate who Mary had murdered. The last time Mary had murdered someone was in a woodwork shop. Someone said something that wasn't to Mary's liking, so he walked over, picked up a chisel, stabbed the inmate in the chest, and then placed the bloodied chisel down on the instructor's desk and said, 'There's one off the roll, Guv.'

Mary was, at the time of writing, one of the few inmates in the country to be told he would never be released from prison.

Night fishing

I was back on nights this week, in the Seg unit. The usual chorus of shouts and lines were being swung between cells. These lines are like improvised fishing lines made from anything the inmate can get hold of. When an item like tobacco is tied to the end and passed out of the window before being swung across to the next cell, it is actually an efficient way of passing stuff. An inmate on the ones can, with co-operation from the others, pass something up to the fours in a matter of minutes.

We see this, of course, and often it's fun to do a spot of fishing of our own. We have a wooden mop handle with a hook on the end, which we stick out of our window – which incidentally only opens a few inches – and use it to pull the line in. Sometimes the item will be confiscated and sometimes we just tie the line off – which is simply to tie it to something solid, so that it appears to be stuck. Then listening in to the inmates arguing among themselves – 'Have you got it yet?' 'No, it's fucking stuck' – can liven up an otherwise dull nightshift. Childish, I know.

Sometimes, if it's a particularly unpleasant inmate either trying to pass or receive, the item will be taken by the officer and replaced with something like a bar of soap. Then the arguments get really nasty. The person receiving thinks he's been had over, while the person passing it thinks he's the one who's been had over and the recipient has kept it but won't admit it.

Occasionally, staff use some of the confiscated items, particularly tobacco, as an incentive for an inmate to do the staff a good turn or give information.

I had just finished tying off yet another line, when I heard my radio. 'P1 needed, O1 to attend immediately.' P1 was the radio call sign for A wing, which was just next door. O1 was Oscar 1, the call sign for the PO, of course. Once O1 replied, I got on my radio and informed P1 that I was on my way to their location. On arriving, the OSG told me that there was an inmate covered in claret in his cell, so I popped up and had a look. It was one of the regular self-harmers who didn't really ever do any damage to himself but liked the attention. His first question to me was, 'Guv, who's O1 tonight?' When I told him, he wasn't best pleased.

He had every right to feel that way when Del turned up, minus his bedside manner. He was even grumpier than usual because he had just made his first brew and hadn't yet had time to drink it because of this. We opened up the cell and asked 'very politely' what seemed to be the problem. It was obvious that the suicide attempt was nothing of the sort. He had cut two fingers on his left hand and liberally smeared the blood around his face for effect. However, the danger with these attention-seekers was that if they didn't get the attention they felt they deserved, they might just up the ante and do something really stupid, whether by accident or design.

Thankfully, the rest of the night was uneventful, aside from a couple of the inmates still arguing over a line that had become inexplicably stuck. What on earth was on the line that warranted such a prolonged and heated discussion, I had no idea. I put the kettle on and tried to drown it out.

Cell fire

When I arrived for tonight's shift, I was told that the 'incident at height' national team were in. These officers are specialists in dealing with any incident at height, such as rooftop demonstrations.

As I walked up through the prison it was like a film set, with an impressive array of kit on display: customised tactical transit vans with monitors, cables leading here and there, floodlights, C & R and climbing gear – and an abundance of testosterone and tea. It was only when I neared the Seg unit that I could actually see what the incident was. Some pissed-off inmate had climbed onto a small roof, though 'roof' is perhaps overstating the case. I doubt it was 10 feet high. I could have knocked him off using a broom, but the powers that be wouldn't allow such draconian methods. Instead, it was far better to get the incident-at-height team from the mainland onto the Isle of Wight at a cost to the taxpayer of many thousands of pounds.

There was, as always, a lot of waiting around. A load of tea was drunk. There was some more waiting around. Finally, the inmate came down of his own accord and he was taken to the block. The incident-at-height team then had to write reams of reports about their turning up, waiting around, drinking tea and going home.

The inmate responsible was put into the 'back cell' – an isolated cell in the Seg unit – with all clothing and personal items removed. Clean prison clothing was issued and, once a manager could be located, he turned up and spoke to him. Tales of woe were spun by the inmate – no doubt about how he wasn't breastfed as a baby, he was an only child and his hamster died when he was six – before the manager instructed staff to relocate the inmate into a 'normal' Seg unit cell and give him back his tobacco, lighter and paperback book.

Once all the staff had disappeared and I had just about finished off the paperwork, the fire alarm went off. It was 1 a.m. The alarm panel indicated that it was in the cell of the prison's most unenthusiastic rooftop demonstrator and unfortunately, when I arrived it was clear it wasn't a false alarm, as I had hoped. There was smoke billowing from the cell.

I called it in, stating the location and confirming the fact that it was real (we received a lot of false alarms). Then I unwound the hose – which for once hadn't been left out ready for use – undid the inundation point in the cell door, a hole that allows us to get water in to the cell in the event of a fire, and inserted the hose. The inmate had helpfully obstructed this with his mattress, and he was pushing it to prevent me from extinguishing the fire, while I was pushing the hose to put the fire out and save his life. However, the only thing I seemed to be achieving was getting my feet wet – the water was just flowing out from underneath his door. There was a lot of smoke – I was coughing and spluttering, and my eyes were stinging and sore – but as long as this pushing and shoving contest continued, I knew he was alive.

Some forty minutes after the alarm was raised, the cavalry arrived in the form of the fire brigade and other prison staff. And it was just as well. I was a wreck, the smoke by now burning my eyes, my lungs gasping for oxygen and my desperate efforts to put out the fire still ongoing. I barely registered what was going on as the fire brigade took over and administered first aid and oxygen to me. I was taken over to the outside hospital's A & E department and spent the night there.*

Lo and behold, it turned out that the inmate had used his book and lighter to start the fire – the very same lighter and book that the manager had instructed the officers to hand back to him.

Problems with the pipework

When I arrived for my night shift, I was given a quick briefing about the day's events. A couple of C & R incidents

---

* I was given the following night off work – just one night – before I was back on the wing.

and one member of staff assaulted, who ended up with a broken jaw. Just another day at the office, then.

Once the briefing was complete, I did the roll check: a couple of blocked observation panels (spyholes, as we preferred to call them), a couple of 'fuck offs', a master masturbator indulging in his favourite pastime and a request from a new inmate on the Seg unit to get a couple of cigarette papers from the cell next door. This request was politely refused. I never pass items on nights. At least, I thought it was a polite refusal. He obviously misheard me, as he let rip with a torrent of abuse and the threat to keep me busy all night long.

Once I completed the obligatory jobs, roll check and the ACCTS, I signed the things that needed signing, ticked the boxes that needed ticking and then signed to say I had signed the things that needed signing and ticked the boxes that needed ticking. I then settled down with a cup of tea and hopes of a quiet night after the other night's unwelcome trip to A & E.

I should have known better. Getting on his cell bell, the new inmate began to ask for anything he could think of that he knew he couldn't have. After the third time, I informed him that he had been nicked for misuse of the emergency cell bell. He was a little displeased to say the least.

I left him shouting insults that sounded anatomically impossible, but after a few minutes he quietened down and instead started tapping the pipes, which ran through the adjoining cells. For me this was only slightly annoying, so I ignored it. The other inmates, however, found it rather more annoying, so they started raising a noise as they began demanding he stop it or else.

Eventually, my patience ran out. I could take it no longer, so I went up and looked through his spyhole. He had made himself comfortable with his mattress on the floor, from where he could tap away merrily on the pipes with his plastic cup. I went through the motions of telling him to stop, even though I knew it was a pointless exercise.

I had a quick think on what to do next. I went into the hotplate area and grabbed one of the paper hats food servers were obliged to wear, then got a big black marker pen and wrote on the front in large capital letters: 'FUCK OFF'. Donning the hat, I returned to his cell, opened the spyhole and stood just far enough back for him to get the full effect.

If I thought he was displeased before, I was in for a rude awakening. He went berserk, yelling threats and smashing up his cell. I put the kettle on and then shredded the hat before making a call to O1, informing him that an inmate I had placed on report for misusing his cell bell was now smashing up his cell. He called for a C & R team. They arrived at the prison a little over an hour later and the inmate was relocated to an isolated back cell. Problem solved.

The next day

Fortunately for me, today's adjudication turned out to be a bit of a farce. The inmates in the neighbouring cells, whom the pipe-tapping arsehole of an inmate had royally pissed off, disputed his version of events, telling the SO they didn't hear me tell the inmate to 'fuck off' (they hadn't realised that the inmate had actually *read* the words). When I reported for duty tonight, I was rather informally asked by the Seg unit SO if I was wearing a white hat. I, of course, told him I never wore a hat while on duty.

Shit: a prison officer's guide

When I hear excrement described as a waste product, I always feel it does a disservice to the enterprising inmates who always manage to find new uses for it. It is often used as a payback threat or warning. A pot of faecal matter would be thrown into the victim's cell and smeared all over their property: photos, bedding, books and any other personal items are instantly destroyed by a liberal coating of crap. This form of warning is an unwritten prison rule that is understood by both staff and inmates: the victim had better be moved off the wing or else.

Its use as a weapon is particularly popular in prison. One poor officer was on the receiving end today. His first shift back from his holidays and, *bang*! He'd barely had time to register the brown faecal mass travelling at great speed towards him. We collared the inmate responsible and when we asked the officer what the hell he'd said to him to provoke it, he replied, 'Fuck all! I've been in Lanzarote for two weeks.'

The victims of such cowardly attacks rarely know why they are on the receiving end. In this case, it turned out that the officer had apparently said 'no' to the inmate (a seemingly innocuous word that inmates hate above all others) before his holidays. While the officer had been sunning it up on the beach, the inmate had been simmering over it.

Those who have meticulously planned their premeditated attack might add unpleasant things such as urine, blood and semen to their projectile, spending several days creating their crappy concoction. Add in the fact that a number of inmates carry diseases such as Hepatitis and HIV – and are happy to collect or purchase quantities of blood and saliva to throw at staff – and it gives a whole new meaning to a potentially lethal cocktail.

Excrement can be fired at an officer passing a cell through the small crack surrounding the door. One particular inmate would hear the officer approaching and this would be his cue. The officer would check the spyhole and, once happy, he would insert the key. The inmate would squat and crap into his hand then throw the resulting mess in the direction of the door.

We don't always catch the people who launch these excrement missiles. Often, the attacks are done from behind or above, and are delivered in some interesting ways. Some choose to crap into a crisp packet and then use it like a 'water' bomb. One enterprising inmate somehow filled a vacuum flask (which, incidentally, we supplied) with his faeces, and then took the glass insert out and launched it into the wing office, with suitably kaleido-scopic results.

It's pretty grim stuff – and certainly isn't mentioned in any job description I've ever read: must be prepared to be literally shat on.

Stripes

An inmate by the name of Leroy walked up behind another inmate on the landing this evening and with three quick slashes, 'striped' his back. Striping is used to wound or warn and is usually done on the buttocks to make life as unpleasant as possible. The lacerations were deep and bloody, and the inmate on the receiving end turned round and shouted, 'You fucking black cunt, you're a fucking dead man walking!'

Now, obviously there's no place for that kind of racist language, of course. And a governor who was passing heard it and said, 'Get that man down the block and nick him for using racist comments.' But there was the small matter of the severe and deep lacerations he'd suffered, so healthcare were on their way to treat him. The governor was adamant that he should be taken to the block immediately for shouting racist remarks and that racism in any form would not be tolerated.

We banged up the wing. Leroy was removed to the Seg unit. The healthcare staff arrived and, with a couple of officers, took the assaulted inmate away to be treated. This wasn't so easy because he was still fuming, his adrenaline obviously still pumping, and the two escorting officers had to manhandle him away. However, no one placed him on report. The general consensus was that if the governor wanted him nicked for using racist language then he should do it.

The wounds were deep and nasty but not life-threatening and they could be managed in-house, which was a blessed relief, because it was nearly time to knock off and nobody really fancied a trip to the outside hospital.

One of the escorting officers, who had been involved in the original assault and had subsequently helped to get the victim to healthcare, was covered in claret. Another officer offered him a clean shirt, which he declined. So it was suggested he go and have a wash and grab some clean uniform from the stores. He again declined but said he would have to go home, as he was a bit shaken by what he had seen. He then phoned his wife to say he was on his way home and that he was covered in blood, but she wasn't to worry as the blood wasn't his. Why he didn't put a clean shirt on was beyond both me and everyone else.

The day we stopped a suicide attempt

I was busy making a cuppa, when the general alarm sounded and all of our radios spewed out: '*Alarm bell, hospital. Alarm bell, hospital. Urgent assistance required!*' This was, as I mentioned earlier, very unusual. The hospital officers take great pride in working with some of the most damaged inmates in the system and they rarely call for assistance. They like to keep things in-house, so if an alarm bell goes off in the hospital, you know it's serious.

We sprinted there, my heart racing, and we clambered up the stairs (why is there never an emergency on the ones?) to the source of the alarm: a cell fire. The trouble with the hospital part of Parkhurst was that the floors and cell doors were all wooden, so any fire was even more serious than in the main part of the prison.

PO Den Shep opened the observation flap and couldn't see anything, but the hospital staff confirmed that the inmate was in the cell. Den shouted to the inmate to get down on the floor. No reply. The smoke was black, thick and acrid. Den shouted again, still no reply. This didn't bode well.

The roof vents were opened, the fire hose made ready and the staff were in place. Den crouched down and cracked the cell door open, again shouting instructions to the inmate (the assumption was that he was going rush out at us), but still nothing. Once the door was opened wide enough, Den crept forwards on his hands and knees. Normally, when a PO is creeping forwards on his hands and knees, he is trying for promotion, but Den was different, a natural leader who always led from the front.

Den was coughing and spluttering his way into the cell, but he still couldn't find the inmate. The cell was being

114

sprayed with water in an attempt to douse the fire, but the thick black smoke made finding the source of the fire impossible. Den finally found a foot under the bed, grabbed it and, using a few choice words to explain the severity of the situation, tried to drag him out. Den was a little over 6 foot tall, weighed 18 stone and was as strong as an ox, but he couldn't get the inmate out from under the bed. He pulled, tugged and swore, but the inmate wouldn't budge. He moved further in and grabbed the wrist then gave an almighty tug or several. Still no joy.

We were all coughing and spluttering by now, so God knows what effect it was having on the two under the bed. Den crept another few inches further in, reached up for his shoulder and then realised what was going on. The inmate had tied a ligature around his neck and to the bed, then rolled over a couple times to tighten the thing in an apparent attempt to strangle himself. Den shouted for a fish – the tool we use for cutting ligatures – but it wasn't up to the job. The ligature was too thick. He shouted for some scissors and they did the trick. The inmate was at last extracted from the cell, with Den really feeling the effects of the smoke inhalation now, and the hospital staff took over.

The inmate made it, but it was seriously touch-and-go. How he survived the cell fire, attempted hanging and Den's rescue attempt is nothing short of miraculous – and even more incredible was the fact that he didn't end up with a neck like a giraffe.

Crap diet

An inmate was moved to a specialist poisons unit at the outside hospital today. He had become extremely ill over the last few days and his poison of choice was his own faeces. This wasn't the first time that he'd been guilty of eating faeces. Nor was it done just for show or to mess with our heads: he'd been caught several times when he was unaware that staff were observing his behaviour. Concerned officers consequently informed both the healthcare team and the psychology department. While we were convinced it was a mental health issue, the psychology department came to the conclusion that it was not a case of coprophagia (the proper name for consuming faeces), but rather it was a discipline issue.★

To be fair, excrement is an incredibly popular tool in the self-harming department. Some inmates are fond of slicing, cutting and scratching themselves and then, rather than applying an antiseptic ointment like Savlon or Germolene, they apply excrement, smearing the wounded area with a liberal coating of faecal matter so that the wound becomes infected and festers.

When visits go wrong

I was working on visits again today. I hated visits – the usual fun and games that came with it – as we had to be switched on as ever to the possibility of things being passed and sugar-fuelled children tearing the place apart. The prison drug dogs were hyperactive, seemingly fun-loving spaniels, always wagging their tails. The kids loved them and were taken in by their playful nature.

Today, one young lad took a shine to a dog, but unfortunately for him the dog indicated the presence of drugs to

★ He was later diagnosed as being mentally ill and transferred to Broadmoor high security psychiatric hospital.

its handler. We took his mum aside and she protested her son's innocence before the tears started to flow. She did, I had to admit, seem convincing and as she broke down, her son piped up and admitted that he and his mates had been smoking 'a little bit of weed – but only the once', and that must be what the dog could smell.

The visit, of course, had to be cancelled* and the mum was furious, screaming at her son about wasting the whole day and all that money on travel for nothing. The dad wasn't too happy either, saying it was our fault this has happened – his son was on drugs because Dad was inside. We get this a lot from inmates: somehow, it's never their fault; we're the ones to blame for depriving a wife of a husband or a child of their father.

Guerilla warfare

There were five of us sitting in the wing office on the threes, when the door suddenly opened. An inmate wearing an improvised balaclava and armed with one of the dry-powder fire extinguishers shouted, 'Cunts!' and proceeded to spray us with the fire extinguisher. Blinded and choking, we stumbled and fumbled our way out of the office, with one officer tripping over the now discarded extinguisher and banging his head on the railings as he went down like a sack of shit. We lifted him up and hit the general alarm. His face was ashen and he was sweating heavily. Healthcare and backup arrived within moments and the wing was

---

* Which is about the limit of our powers with civilians. If we suspected she was carrying drugs or a strip search was required, we would have to contact the police.

quickly banged up, but we didn't catch the culprit. We did, however, have a good idea who it was and as was our custom, we would let him know we knew in our own very unofficial but effective way.

Off the lead

As I was leaving at the end of my shift, there was a huge commotion just outside the car park. Carl, the security SO (the one who'd instructed us to search for 'amphibians'), had been knocked off his bicycle by a German shepherd dog that suddenly appeared out of nowhere. The owner, an off-duty dog handler, ran up and got the thing under control, but Carl was shaken and had a nasty bite to his left leg.

The next day

When everyone found out what had happened in the car park the night before, they asked the dog handler if the poor dog was all right and hoped that his vaccinations were all up to date after taking a bite of something as hazardous and unappetising as Carl.

Karma is a bitch

The inmate who we were certain had attacked us with the fire extinguisher has started being careless. Somehow, he lost a training shoe out of the window today, after the insoles of his shoes went missing just a few days ago. And would you believe it? His name was somehow left off the reception list and he's been the last to get unlocked all week, which in turn meant he was last in line for the phone, the library and to put his name on the gym list, so he missed out. Justice takes many forms and karma really is a bitch.

Undressing to impress

I was doing the labour movement board, basically marking each inmate off as they went to work, and one new inmate walked right past me eating food, which was a no-no. As he was new to the wing, I called out, 'Smith! No eating and no food.'

My rather gentle approach fell on deaf ears, so this time I went louder: '*Smith!*'

Now he heard me.

He turned round and shouted, 'Don't you shout my fucking name!'

'*Smith!*' I shouted again.

He said, 'Do that again and I'll kno—'

'*Smiiith!*' I yelled.

That was it. He went berserk, with threats to cut my throat and a whole host of other very unpleasant things. He also began moving towards me, which I hoped was just showboating for the crowd that had now gathered and were enjoying the show, so I stood my ground. He moved quickly and then went to pull his shirt off over his head, no doubt to impress and intimidate. All the while he was telling his audience that this 'fucking screw was going down'.

It was all going well until he got stuck in his shirt. He hadn't undone enough buttons and he'd got it stuck over his ears. He was bent over, tangled up and frantically trying to fight his way out of the unruly shirt. It was like watching a drunk trying to get undressed. The once violent threats now became nothing more than muffled moans. He eventually got one arm free but the other, like his head, was still buried inside his shirt.

Fortunately, by the time he had finally extricated himself from his public wardrobe malfunction, he was red-faced, sweating and breathing heavily. His once captive audience were in hysterics and he skulked back on to the wing with as much dignity as he could muster. I was just relieved that a shedload of paperwork had been avoided.

Colour me yellow

Woody was an inmate located in the HCC and was a loner and not in the best of health. Today, he looked even worse than usual. During association he was sitting in his usual corner, when one of the officers noticed that he was quieter than normal and looked slightly off colour, with a definite yellow tinge. He asked one of the hospital officers to take a look. The immediate diagnosis was potentially serious: jaundice. He was taken to see the doctor, who was a little perplexed, because though his skin had a definite yellow tinge, with jaundice the whites of the eyes would be yellow, too, and Woody's appeared normal.

The doctor took him in to one of the examination rooms and asked him to remove his shirt. He was slightly surprised to see that the only yellow bits on the patient were his hands and face. Woody admitted that he had nicked a yellow highlighting pen and then coloured his face and hands, hoping that this would get him seen quicker by the doctor. And he certainly was seen quickly, even if I didn't think the doctor would be in a hurry to see him quickly again.

The day an officer died

The assault this evening on two officers was as close to murder as it is possible to get without going all the way. One officer actually died and had to be revived while in hospital. The attack was premeditated and ruthless in its execution.

The ambush was planned because an inmate had decided that one particular officer deserved a fucking good kicking. The officer concerned was one of the longer-serving ones, hugely experienced and even more hugely respected. He was old-school through and through. If an inmate was entitled to something, he would move heaven and earth to make sure that he had it; however, if an inmate wasn't entitled to something, he would move heaven and earth to make sure he didn't get it. He would say no only when the word was called for; everything was black and white, yes or no, rules is rules, absolutely no ambiguity. He was honest, fair and professional, and most inmates, like his colleagues, respected him. But you are always going to have inmates who hate the word no.

The whole attack was meticulously planned, almost military in its precision, with the aim to split up the officers on duty and pounce on their prey. This particular evening was chosen because it was library night. One officer would be off the wing, taking inmates to the library, two officers would be on the threes, observing association time, and two officers – one of whom was the intended victim – would be on the ones.

As soon as the library party left, the plan was set in motion with a few raised voices in the association room. The observing officers intervened and tried to calm the arguing inmates. This had now served to distract two of the four officers on the wing.

The next part of the plan was to separate the two remaining officers on the ones (the inmates hadn't realised that there was actually a third officer on the ones, an officer who had arrived from another wing to pick up some laminating sheets). This was easy enough. An inmate went to the office and asked for his cell at the other end of the landing to be unlocked. This would then leave the intended victim either in the office alone, or at the other end of the ones, depending on which officer went to unlock the cell door. It was the intended victim who went to unlock the door and that was all they needed – just a few moments when the officer was alone.

The attack was fast and savage. The four inmates surrounding him were like a pack of frenzied animals, and they quickly and brutally beat him. Blows rained down, the bloodlust was up and within seconds, the officer was down. Kicks, punches, blows from socks filled with pool balls, chair and table legs, anything to hand – even his dropped radio, which he had vainly attempted to use to call for assistance, was used as a weapon.

The other two staff on the ones were on the scene quickly. One was a gentle old soul, not unlike the Mr Barrowclough character in *Porridge*, whose non-confrontational approach to the job made him, in the eyes of the assailants, a non-threat. He was physically restrained and told in no uncertain terms to fuck off and keep out of it. The other officer, however, was an ex-squaddie with balls the size of coconuts, who hit the alarm bell and grabbed the first inmate in an attempt to get to the officer under attack.

The trouble was that other inmates on the wing only saw an officer remonstrating with an inmate, so they decided to get involved. Now, the four initial assailants had grown to a dozen or more and the backup responding to the alarm bell walked into a mass brawl. Three officers from the Seg unit arrived first, to the sight of two officers down: the intended victim was in a strange bent and twisted position, and appeared lifeless. His eyes rolled back, he was covered in claret and blood was running from one ear. It was quickly decided to make a beeline for the officer who had gone to his aid, who by now had been beaten to a bloody pulp, was covered in claret and was convulsing.

Two of the four initial attackers were immediately taken to the block under restraint, while other inmates on the landings were now shouting obscenities and threats, throwing things and inflaming the situation. A pack mentality had taken hold, with minor skirmishes between officers and inmates. The inmates were determined to put on a show of superficial unity.

Once the wing was swamped with staff and dog handlers, order was tentatively restored. The scab lifters arrived and immediately called for ambulances. Life-saving intervention was necessary and after what seemed to be an absolute age, the paramedics arrived and took the two officers to A & E. Staff got them through the gates pronto.

After the ambulances had left, the door-kicking, the threats and the shouting from the inmates began. The usual way to deal with this was to ignore what we could and wait. After all, the inmates were behind their doors and weren't going anywhere. There were two ACCTs and one of them was shouting the odds, so only one needed checking. The dog handlers riled up their canine companions so they barked and growled. Electricity and water were turned off in the cells. C & R teams kitted up and waited.

After a good couple of hours, when the inmates had eventually run out of steam, the C & R teams went in and, one at a time, removed those attackers who had been immediately identified. The advantage of having a sister site – Albany, a separate prison, which we'll get to in Part III – was that there were two Seg units available. Both were quickly filled and a cautious order was restored.

The two officers who were attacked were immediately rushed into the A & E department, and the ex-squaddie was taken straight into the operating theatre because of his severe head injuries. He actually died on the operating table for a minute or so and had to be resuscitated. The other officer was unconscious but by some miracle alive.

Both officers eventually returned to work after a long period off, but the mental and physical after-effects remained with them throughout their time with the service.

PART II:

The Twenty-First Century Prison Service

CHAPTER 7

Experience

By 2002, I was coming up to ten years in the service. On the one hand, you could say I was an experienced officer, but on the other, as I worked alongside officers with thirty years in the service, you could also say I still had plenty to learn. I was coming towards the end of my time on A wing – a tough, uncompromising place to work, but it was often rewarding work, with a good sense of camaraderie among staff. Or, in plainer-speaking terms, it was 'a good crew on a shit wing'.

The day a fellow officer dropped me in it

It hasn't happened often, but on a couple of occasions I have been put at risk by my fellow officers. Today, I walked into a situation that had potential disaster written all over it.

I'd just arrived and was in the back office hanging my coat up, when I heard the unmistakable sound of glass being smashed. I rushed out of the office and straight into a circle of inmates. It was like a scene in a school playground when two kids are having a fight surrounded by a circle of spectators. I was standing in the middle among the shards of broken glass from a smashed flask and then, just as the PO turned up, an inmate collapsed.

The PO tended to the now semi-conscious inmate and I tried to work out what the hell had happened. Looking around and then up, I noticed Jizzy Jack standing on the twos, right above me. Jizzy Jack got his rather unfortunate nickname owing to the fact that when he was working at the prison in a different role, he had been caught vigorously masturbating on the job.

I asked him, 'Did you see what happened?'

He replied, 'It was Miller.'

Miller was a violent criminal from Bristol and when I spotted him in the crowd, I noticed that his hand was bleeding. As the troops arrived, I said to him, 'Miller, you're bleeding, mate.' Now everyone knew it was him. As the wing was being banged up, Miller attacked an officer and was 'wrapped up' – prison speak for when we physically restrain an inmate, an officer on each arm applying wrist locks and an officer controlling the head – and removed to the block.

It was only afterwards that I realised Jizzy Jack had seen the whole thing and all he had to do was hit the alarm bell behind him. He didn't even have to move; he just had to turn round. But he didn't. Instead, he watched me walk into a potentially volatile situation without saying or doing a thing.

Instinct

This morning, I hit the alarm bell on A wing when I had no real reason to do so – but something just didn't feel right. I was on the fours and had just banged up an inmate, when I thought I heard something. It was a dull thud and looking down to the other landings, I couldn't see anything. More worryingly, I couldn't hear anything, either, so I decided to go down to the ones. When I reached the twos, I looked down and noticed that the main office door was open, but no officer was in there. I immediately hit the bell.

I reached the ones and, just before I got to the wing office, I saw that the staff tea-room door was open and there were two officers frantically restraining an inmate up against the wall in the corner. He had just attacked another inmate, who was now sparko on the floor in a pool of claret. The officers couldn't move; one wrong move to raise the alarm, and the inmate would have broken free and in all probability assaulted them. They could only hold on and hope. The troops arrived just at that moment and I pointed them towards the tea room.

'Jail craft' is by far the greatest skill that any officer can have, but it's a particular skill that's not taught at the training college because it's one that can't really be taught. Picking up little fluctuations in behaviour, reading body language, feeling the atmosphere – jail craft isn't a tangible thing. It's a skill that is often acquired over a long period of time – like osmosis, it's slowly absorbed – but it's also dependent on the individual officer's capacity to acquire it. I've seen fairly new officers pick up subtle behavioural traits and nuances that indicate trouble just round the corner, but I've also seen experienced officers not notice the glaringly obvious when it's right in front of them.

After ten years in the job, these instincts were certainly coming more naturally to me, but they had been slowly acquired over all the many hours I'd spent on the landings. If I had hit the bell and got it hopelessly wrong today, I wouldn't have been able to answer with anything other than, 'It just didn't feel right', which risked me looking like an idiot. But I'd learnt to trust my gut.

Another skill that's acquired is learning to let the inmates do the work for you. Someone hit the alarm bell to piss off the staff the other day – or so he thought. For us it was easy. The troops arrived and we banged up the wing. Those inmates who want association, showers and to make phone calls weren't happy about it. So we had an extra unplanned tea break before we unlocked and in the meantime, the inmate who hit the alarm got a warning from the pissed-off inmates. Basically, they take care of it in-house, away from our prying eyes, while we get an extra tea break.

Assault

An inmate assaulted three staff today, having returned to the wing after being sent to the Seg unit for making threats to assault staff. This wasn't the first time it had happened with this particular inmate.

Losing your keys

I met the new deputy governor of the prison today while he was being shown around the wings. He cut quite an impressive figure and seemed keen to hear what we had to say and to make changes. He was like a breath of fresh air, to be honest. I learnt in the staff room later, however, that he was only going to be there for six months.

There was some drama around a key going missing. Anyone who's ever lost their house keys knows what the panic is like, the unhelpful comments like 'where was the last place you had them?' and the worry about whose hands they're in now. Well, that kind of panic is amplified many times over when a key goes missing in a prison. The key itself unlocked a door that hid plumbing pipework, but losing any key in prison is serious, as it could be fashioned into opening any lock in expert hands. We were looking all over for it, turning the place upside down and worrying about which inmate had got his hands on it. The drama was finally resolved when the key was found in an office drawer, instead of where it should have been, in the key safe. Typical!

Trafficking

An officer was suspended today on suspicion of trafficking tobacco. This is without doubt one of the very worst things that an officer can do. Trafficking is the bringing in of unauthorised items ranging from drugs to phones, and pornography to cigarettes. Even something as innocuous as biscuits, as we'll see in this case.

Trafficking is abhorrent in any shape or form. In our job, we are trusted and required to be virtuous and inhabit the moral high ground. Prison officers should have a degree of integrity and honesty; though as George Bernard Shaw said, 'Virtue is insufficient temptation.'

Trafficking is dangerous and is one of the very few things that officers will not tolerate in any shape or form, and they will have no hesitation in reporting anyone found doing it.★

Trafficking seems to happen more now because new officers coming into the service are paid a hell of a lot less

---

★ And trust me, this means it's serious. We don't normally grass each other up, preferring to sort out any problem face to face, with trafficking one of the only exceptions.

than us, with smaller pensions, which provides a financial incentive. New officers are also often young and naive, and many don't seem to like confrontation.

Unfortunately, it's not just done by the odd bent screw. The prison service employs a vast number of 'civvies', who pack out the prison car park during the week, and in my time Civvy Street smugglers have included teachers, chaplains, shop instructors (who oversee inmates working), healthcare staff and even a doctor, who was once escorted from the prison in handcuffs by the police.

The trouble with trafficking is that it puts people at risk. Our integrity is compromised and, once an officer has been pulled into it, it can have no end. The officer caught today was an example of how easily a gullible and dishonest member of staff can get sucked in to trafficking. And it all started with a seemingly harmless packet of biscuits.

The officer was fairly new, just a few months in the job, and it was obvious he was one of life's panickers. He was nervous and lacking in confidence, and always struggled with the job, but he would never ask for help or advice. To be frank, he gave off the very distinctive aroma of fear. The staff could smell it and, much worse, the inmates could smell it.

The difference was that the staff tried. We offered advice, explained things and led by example, but time and again he fucked up. He was the cleaning officer on a shift a few months ago and as such he was responsible for collecting the meal trolley from the kitchen, loading the hotplate and making sure that things were in order. The cons knew that he was a victim ripe for exploitation. And when he was suitably and easily distracted, the inmates saw their chance and 'half-inched' several packets of biscuits.

For most officers, this would be a simple problem to solve, but for him it was a catastrophic fuck-up. When the inmates came down and collected their meals, they wanted their biscuits. And when those biscuits weren't forthcoming, the inmates got loud and threatening, demanding their 'fucking biscuits'. They were entitled to biscuits just the same as 'every fucker else', they said, and they wouldn't be leaving the hotplate until they got their fucking biscuits. And so it went on.

Rather than call for assistance or, as a last resort, hit the alarm bell, he kept quiet, not wanting to let his colleagues know that he had once again fucked up. And instead he did the most stupid thing he could have done: he promised to get them some biscuits. One of the unwritten rules is that you never promise an inmate anything.

True to his word, he got them their biscuits. The trouble was that he bought them from Tesco with his own money and handed each of the inmates a packet the next day. He was now well and truly screwed, and the inmates knew it. He had trafficked, and the Tesco biscuit wrappers were proof. Those biscuits had now been turned into bargaining chips and over the next few days, he was asked to bring in a couple of magazines, then a packet of cigarettes, then phones, and so it went on.

Initially, he was paid – and paid reasonably well. However, this was only while they reeled him in, hook, line and sinker. Once they had him where they wanted him, he was apparently paid next to nothing before finally being paid fuck all. If he brought the stuff in, they wouldn't grass him up. It wasn't long before he was trafficking anything from biscuits to phones, and all because he panicked. He got caught today bringing cigarettes in and would almost certainly lose his job.

Saving lives

It was a busy and bloody one today. An inmate smashed his cell up, cutting himself in the process, then wrote, 'Fuck off, you cunts' in blood on the wall. Charming. He was removed to the HCC, where he started vomiting blood. Turned out he had a history of eating and swallowing glass and razors, and the doctor was called.

Another inmate attempted to hang himself in the HCC. As I've said, the hospital staff like to deal with their problems in-house, so an alarm bell from here is usually something serious. However, no staff were available to attend, which left only one PO and another inmate to try to save his life. He survived, but only thanks to the quick-thinking and heroic work of the pair of them.

Playing by the rules

I returned to work after a week off to find out that another officer had been suspended. If I thought I was going to be able to ease my way back into work gently after some time off, I was in for a rude awakening. An alarm bell went off and when I arrived, it was to something like a scene out of *Bugsy Malone* – a food fight among a group of inmates. And while it certainly wasn't good-natured, it was definitely one of the gentler attacks I've been called to (though no less messy, of course).

We had difficulty banging up the wing later on. There are three tiers of prisoner: those on basic, standard and enhanced regimes, with basic having the fewest privileges and enhanced the most, depending on the prisoner's behaviour and willingness to work. The basics today were not happy. An inmate on basic gets a limited time out of their cell to collect meals, shower and the rest. They get no association time and no TV. They were pissed off because they weren't unlocked to fill their flasks up with hot water, which was in line with the rules.

The trouble starts because some staff, usually the more experienced ones, stick to the rules, but new young officers faced with an inmate who kicks the door, shouts the odds and demands his hot water often let them out to keep the peace and avoid confrontation. It's only a bit of water, after all. We come along the next day and say no, and the basic inmates get annoyed, saying, 'We were allowed out yesterday.' They then wind each other up and goad each other into causing chaos – and they were working together to try to intimidate staff now.

This was when things could get dangerous on the wing, when the inmates start working together and hunting as a pack, and the tension in the air was palpable. Thankfully, we had a good crew on today and we didn't back down.

Not that it mattered in the end. The governors caved in and allowed the basics out to get water, two at a time. It seemed to me that this set a terrible precedent and meant the basics now knew what to do to get a result, which in turn made the officers' lives even more difficult.

The emergency code

Today, I had the dubious pleasure of standing toe to toe with a pissed-off inmate, recently arrived from HMP Whitemoor, who threatened to rip my 'fucking head off'. He explained in particularly menacing terms that he had 'already assaulted four screws at his last gaff' and unless I got him down the block, I'd be the fifth – and the first here. When I called down for assistance, the only other officer told me that he was on the phone. I told him in no uncertain terms, 'Officer on the ones!'

He took the hint and, with my adrenaline rocketing and my relief at the sight of some backup, we moved the big angry lump to the block. I later did a check on the inmate and was able to confirm that he was as good as his word: he had assaulted four officers at HMP Whitemoor.*

The left-handed letter

The infamous and ever popular 'left-handed letter' was a technique mastered by some of the less-than-courageous officers. A handwritten note would suddenly appear in the wing's mailbox making threats towards a particular officer – to kill or pot them. The gist of it was always the same: get that officer off the wing for his own safety. The suspicion was always that the less-than-courageous officer had written the note himself – using the non-dominant hand in a rather feeble attempt to disguise his or her own handwriting – because they wanted off the wing but didn't have the courage to say so.

And then there was the other popular approach among some officers who really didn't like wing work and dealing with prisoners, in which they would deliberately provoke a situation that required them to be removed from the wing. This option at least allowed them to save face and still look tough – even if it was away from the front line of the wing.

---

* After this incident, we decided that if any of us shouted, 'Officer on the ones!' it was deemed to be an emergency.

I've known officers with years in the job – and I'm talking double-digit years – never having worked on a wing.

So it didn't come as much of a surprise today when the PO gathered us round and told us that many staff refused point-blank to work on A wing, threatening to go on the sick if detailed there. The PO spoke to us today because we had all done our time on the most challenging wing and the time for moving on was fast approaching. He told us he'd understand if any of us wanted a transfer off the wing and he wanted to know how we felt. We all said the same thing: it's a good crew on a shit wing. We all agreed we'd stay.

Knowing the limit

There was a rumour going around the prison that one of the officers in the Seg unit had been sent home during mid-week ED because he'd cracked up. This was confirmed today. Apparently, the officer had been in the office one minute, seemingly working normally, and the next minute he burst into tears, got up and walked out of the Seg without saying a word – or even taking his coat with him. As I mentioned earlier, the Seg unit crew were the 'hardmen' of the prison staff. They dealt with the most difficult inmates when they were at their most difficult, and the Seg unit officer had been there, done that, got the T-shirt and then some. It was proof that even for the most experienced, toughest prison officers, everyone has their limit. Everyone has their breaking point.

Apparently, Parkhurst could only run with thirty-one non-effectual staff, which was officers and uniformed grade who didn't, for whatever reason, work on the wing and so didn't work directly with inmates. At present, we had sixty-three! Nine officers and one SO had requested and been granted a transfer interview at our sister site, Albany. Despite those of us on A wing choosing to stay, a lot of staff had had enough of Parkhurst. I, like many other staff, was going in to work hoping against hope that I would get through the shift without getting hurt. Albany was a softer option, with a lot less violence, and I couldn't really blame some of these officers for wanting to get out.

Cannon fodder

Things seemed to come to a head today. Four staff were assaulted in the Seg unit, with smashing up and, more unpleasantly, inmates shitting up en masse. One officer had two broken ribs and we lost twelve cells in there (they were damaged and out of use). The fire brigade was also called because inmates were setting a number of fires during lunchtime bang-up. What a day.

After all the trouble in the Seg unit, one of the managers had apparently said, 'Remember, lads, you're the cannon fodder.' I hoped this was just gossip, because comments like that really don't help.

The incident made it into the papers, but they mistakenly said that no staff were injured.

Prison review

Two more fires were started outside A wing today. I was getting to be a dab hand at firefighting. These fires were started by setting a sheet or something similar on fire then throwing them out of the window. Many of the inmates considered it great fun to set the outside alight and then watch either us or, if it was more serious, the fire brigade put them out. The clear-up afterwards could be risky, too, as the wrong cleaner would potentially be in the firing line for shit-parcels or other projectiles.

The Board of Visitors consisted of an independent group of volunteers who visited prisons to make sure the proper standards were being maintained. They appeared on the news and in the press stating that Parkhurst was woefully understaffed and the whole situation was basically a disaster waiting to happen. Personally, I usually found these visits to be pretty inaccurate – though they weren't wrong about the staffing levels. They seemed to get a lot of information from prisoners and took them at their word, rather than get a more rounded and accurate picture. And when you actually think about it, any prison is a disaster waiting to happen.

No room in the Seg unit

An officer placed two inmates on report, but a PO then asked if the officer could withdraw the 'nickings' because the Seg was so busy. Inmates were now seemingly allowed to get away scot-free if they broke the prison rules simply because the Seg was busy. We were failing in the most basic things and yet it was condoned.

Catch 22

Many of us were annoyed to learn today that we have lost annual leave hours because our leave requests were rejected owing to staff shortages and we're not allowed to carry over more than seventy hours.

Police investigations

Today, I was interviewed by CID (Criminal Investigation Department) regarding a cell fire dating back to almost a year ago. I'd dealt with so many cell fires since then I could barely recall the incident in question, but thankfully we have the notebooks we fill out daily as a record of the day's events to jog our memories. For this one, I'd discovered it, called it in and helped to try to find the cell's occupier. We'd eventually found him in the shower! Why the police had suddenly shown an interest in it, I had no idea.

The day an inmate punched me

We were busy getting the inmates in from the exercise yard today, when one of them decided to use the wing phone on the ones. The time for phone calls was during association and certainly not now, so I politely asked the inmate to finish off as it was now bang up. He was new on the wing, and he did all the right things and made all the right noises: put his hand up, acknowledged me – and then carried on.

I banged up my landing and he was still on the phone, so I dropped down to the ones and now told him, rather than asked him, to finish off. His reply was instant: 'I'm talking to my mum, you muggy cunt.'

His mum must be so proud, I thought, before I shouted down to the office to switch off the phones. With the phone now out of commission, the inmate went fucking ballistic, threatening me with all sorts of unpleasant things. I escorted him up to his cell on the twos and, once we got there, I told him in no uncertain terms: 'When I say off the phone, I mean off the phone, *now*.'

And then suddenly, out of nowhere, *smack*! He punched me so hard on my jaw I could see stars. Fortunately, this punch had been witnessed by another officer. Unfortunately, the other officer happened to be the invertebrate known as Jizzy Jack. Despite him actually seeing what had happened, I still had to shout at him to hit the bell. He didn't; he just carried on walking.

I now had two choices: I could either hit the bell that my assailant was standing in front of, or I could get to the other end of the landing and hit that bell. I reasoned that if I moved away from him, he would think I was scared shitless and give chase, so I shoved him out of the way and hit the bell behind him. The response was immediate, no thanks to Jizzy Jack.

One of the inmates who was cleaning the landing had witnessed what had happened and was able to back up my version of events. The PO then tore Jizzy a spare one. His reputation was now in shreds – if it wasn't already. A bottleless officer was both a danger and a liability.

The next day

The adjudication today was, thankfully, a pretty clear-cut affair. The inmate pleaded not guilty to assaulting me, but I had my own version of events, witnesses and a swollen jaw on my side as evidence. He was found guilty, which meant he was to be kept in the block on CC (cellular confinement) for a period of time before being transferred out or moved to another wing.

That was the theory, at least. In reality, he was put back on my wing.

The lack of regime

There was a controlled unlock at teatime, again owing to a lack of staff. A controlled unlock involves only letting a few inmates out at a time. It used to be something we did a lot more regularly, and would mean between four and six inmates at a time, though the numbers have crept up over the years. A dozen, then a couple of dozen, and then whole landings and more, as the governors increasingly don't like to upset the inmates.★

The inmates weren't happy about it today and there were the usual moans, but there was little else we could do with our staffing numbers. A small group of inmates in particular were extremely unhappy about the regime – or rather the lack of regime at the moment. There were mutterings of a refusal to bang up and once again, we had to move our personal belongings off the wing, just in case. This was becoming a bit of a serious and regular occurrence. Our coats, bags and the like would be put next door in the education department's cloakroom, which was attached to A wing, so that if – or more likely *when* – the wing went up and we had to make a hasty exit, we would be able to retrieve our personal belongings.

Hostages

We had a hostage situation today, which doesn't happen often. Two inmates took another one hostage, threatening to cut off his ears. In these situations we had a procedure to

---

★ I have worked with some new officers who have never done a controlled unlock, nor even really know what one is.

follow. When an officer responds to such a situation, he or she wouldn't rush down the stairs or use the radio within earshot of other inmates, unless there was an imminent threat to life. The officer would go down to the office, inform the other officers and phone the control room to report it. The alarm or radio wouldn't be used, as you don't want the other inmates to get wind of what is going on and start adding to the chaos.

The protocol was followed today and the wing was banged up. The inmates in the cells either side of the hostage situation were cleared. A C & R team in kit, with a door jack (a tool for breaking down a door – or we could remove a metal plate to open the door outwards), were ready to rush in and the negotiators were sent in.

On some occasions, the hostage has actually been in cahoots with his captors and they've done it just to piss us off. Today, these three were doing just that. They kept the staff at bay, busy and on duty for an extra few hours, while they wanted nothing more than to piss about and finish their hooch. They came out one at a time, each shouting the odds, and they were moved to the block.

Shitty mix-ups

I arrived today to an inmate smashing up his cell and getting stuck into the plumbing, and his cell was now flooding. He'd even smashed the observation panel. We removed him to the back cells in the Seg unit, where he continued his handiwork, kicking the door and threatening to ram his head against the wall. He then proceeded to shit-up (dirty protest), which, given that there was already another dirty protestor on the Seg at the time, literally made for some dirty work.

Now, all I'll say here is that, on occasion, accidents do occur and mistakes sometimes happen. And it just so happens that, on more than one occasion, when a couple of inmates have been on a dirty protest at the same time, they have been taken out of their shit-smeared cells to have a shower. Once they emerge from the shower all clean and fresh, they are given clean clothing and then 'accidentally' put in each other's cells. While their own poo may well be delightfully fragrant and stir in the inmate a certain pride in the quality of their own dirty work, wallowing in another inmate's shit doesn't inspire the same enthusiastic feelings. Let's just say they tend to be a little less than impressed with their accidental relocation.

Quiet, please!

A civilian librarian was escorted out of the prison today. She'd apparently been having sex with more than one inmate.

Something's brewing

A lot of hooch was found over the weekend during a wing spin and today we received information that a lot of the inmates were tooled up. We found three empty fire extinguishers this morning, plus the remains of tool-making equipment, otherwise known as weapons. Hooch + weapons = the potential for disaster.

Banged up

There were more moans and veiled threats from inmates about no association again today. The lack of staff means they can't have association – we just wouldn't be able to cope with it. Keeping the inmates cooped up to simmer and stew about it felt a bit like a time bomb waiting to go off.

Party time

There was a hooch party on A wing today. These don't happen often, but on occasion a load of hooch might be brewed for something like a birthday party or someone about to leave. It's usually half a dozen inmates in a cell drinking and trying to keep things low-key (ha!). Nine times out of ten any rowdiness is kept in check by other inmates. They really don't want someone spoiling for a fight wandering around the landing, so they police it themselves.

We usually realise what's going on and we are aware of the fact that they have lookouts in place, ready to give the informal drinking club a warning of any approaching officer. While the party's going on, the skill is in watching and waiting. Intervene at the wrong moment with half a dozen pissed inmates and you might have a mass brawl or even a riot on your hands. As long as we know it's going on, we can deal with it – when we decide. We would normally wait until bang up if possible, and then get them one on one and place them on report.

Today, the inmates were pissed and fire extinguishers were let off, which meant we had to intervene, but thankfully there wasn't any real trouble and we managed to get them banged up OK.

We then had to spin the wing for the hooch. Surprise, surprise, we found nothing. The expression 'barn doors and horses' sprang to mind. After the search, a couple of us were asked if we had come across any 'compromising' pictures of a female officer that had apparently been taken some years ago and were now doing the rounds. It might have made our searching a bit more thorough if we'd known who it was.

Resilience

It's amazing how routine and everyday putting out fires as part of the job has become. A fire started in the association room a couple of days ago, which we managed to put out using the fire extinguishers, and then yesterday there was another fire outside A wing, which meant we had to evacuate the wing.

I learnt today that one of the officers is now on long-term sick, after an inmate made threats to cut her throat (by drawing his finger across his throat while looking directly at her). Now, while this was undoubtedly upsetting for her, threats of violence are, I'm afraid to say, part and parcel of the job. We each cope with these things in our own way and unfortunately for her, she couldn't cope with that, which, when the prison is so short-staffed, puts an extra burden on the rest of us.

This officer eventually returned to a cushy non-wing job before leaving the service.

Race relations

An inmate wanted to see the race relations officer as a matter of urgency today. Race relations were a hot topic at the moment and incidents were attended to quickly. The race relations officer, who was attending to another inmate, was eventually relieved by another officer, which involved a lot of swapping around, so he could attend to the urgent problem. It turned out that the inmate wanted to know how to get hairbands.

A double whammy

It was bedlam today at the prison. An inmate attempted to hang himself in the Seg unit while also setting fire to the cell – a popular double whammy with some inmates – and an officer unlocked the cell door to fight the fire and saved the screaming inmate. However, the PO reprimanded the officer at the top of his voice in front of other members of staff and the fire brigade. The ones landing had to be evacuated and on opening one of the cell doors, an inmate grabbed the SO around the throat and attempted to strangle her. The inmate was eventually pulled off, and six staff had to go to the outside hospital suffering from smoke inhalation and injuries.

Opening the cell door is a judgement call: if you are going to put yourself or anyone else at risk, it's a no-no; the only time to open it would be to try to save the life of the inmate – the very inmate who started the fire in the first place – without putting yourself or others at risk.

Inmates policing the inmates

A prisoner came up to me today while I was on the landing. 'Guv,' he said, 'some CDs have been half-inched from my peter.'

Rather than going through the hassle of trying to find the CDs myself, I popped down to the ones landing and wrote on the wing noticeboard that there would be a delay in unlocking this afternoon owing to a complete wing spin to find the stolen items – and anything else that might turn up. As expected, one of the pissed-off big boys on the wing came up to me and asked what was going on. He, along with a fair few other inmates, obviously didn't want the wing-spinning. I told him that some CDs had been stolen and if they weren't found then a spin would commence. It was a bluff, but a bluff that paid off, because, lo and behold, within twenty minutes the inmate's CDs had been returned with no questions asked.

The bigger picture

When I arrived for my night shift, a rooftop demonstration was under way. The officer I was relieving filled me in about what had happened the day before. Apparently, an officer had refused point-blank to work on D wing and even after being given a direct order to work there, he still refused and was then escorted to the gate. Rather than being disciplined, the officer had been given special leave to calm himself down and get his thoughts together.

As for the rooftop demonstration, no one seemed to have a clue what it was actually all about. No demands had been made, so maybe 'demonstration' was lending the incident more gravitas than it actually deserved. An inmate had somehow got onto a roof of the security department while he was being escorted and he was now on the roof having a whale of time. He was taking slates off the roof and throwing them at anything that moved. The trouble was that the security department offices below him held all sorts of classified information: prisoner records, files, evidence and God knows what else. Half the prison staff weren't privy to what was actually in the security department, so if the inmate gained access, the situation would be serious.

C & R teams were deployed both inside the building and out. Trained negotiators were met with periods of silence then profanities and then even more slates, thrown like frisbees at anything that moved or spoke. The stand-off continued well into the evening. Not that the staff minded. They were getting paid the standard 'tornado rate' for the incident.*

I was listening to the radio transmissions at about 1 a.m., when one of the governors came across the radio instructing the staff to make sure the ladder was in place and secure. Further orders were given to clear the immediate area of any rubbish or debris, to prevent the inmate from hurting himself. I received a phone call to get a cell ready, as the inmate had now agreed to come down.

This 'agreement' had been reached only on the inmate's terms, which he had laid down to the governor. He wanted a hot meal and a shower, he was not to be 'back celled'

---

* 'Tornado' is what the media would call the specialist riot-trained officers. They are the guys in black flame-retardant overalls with shields and blue helmet, who get 'kitted up' like this to deal with trouble and get a special rate of pay.

(an isolated cell at the back of the Seg) and he could have certain items fetched from his cell. The governor had capitulated and agreed to his terms and conditions.

The staff were now in the process of tidying up the mess and potentially hazardous debris, lest the poor, tired inmate hurt himself. The C & R commander was despatched to the prison kitchens to prepare a hot meal. I received a phone call from Del saying he was on his way to collect me and that we were to go to the inmate's cell to pick up those promised items: tobacco, cigarette papers, toiletries, slippers and a couple of books, one of which, ironically, was the autobiography of Fred Dibnah, the Bolton-born steeplejack.

Once the inmate was off the roof, cuffed and escorted to the block, he was locked in the shower area. His freshly cooked meal arrived, as did Del and I with his promised items. He got out of the shower and into his clean kit wearing a shit-eating, gloating grin.

The governor, however, pleased with a job well done in bringing the inmate to safety, didn't seem overly concerned that the inmate was actually taking the piss. With a little over £32,000 worth of damage done to the roof, plus the cost of deploying C & R teams on the tornado rate, there was, in our eyes, nothing to be pleased about. But the governor seemed to see things differently. It must, I reasoned, be one of those 'bigger picture' things that governors were always telling me I was missing.

Only so many hours in the week . . .

The shortage in staff had already seen many of us working TOIL (Time Off In Lieu) hours, which were hours worked in addition to our usual duties to cover the shortfall, meaning some officers were accumulating huge amounts of hours. The governors soon twigged that we would have to take this time off eventually, thus compounding the problem of not having enough staff. So contracted supplementary hours were introduced, which basically meant we could volunteer to work extra hours, up to a maximum of nine per week – even though many more were needed. Volunteering to work more hours at the prison at this point didn't exactly seem appealing to many of us and I preferred to keep well out of it.

Jizzy Jack strikes again!

The ASO (Acting Senior Officer) was assaulted today, hit with the telephone. Jizzy Jack witnessed the whole thing but again didn't hit the bell. How he had managed to escape discipline and still be in a job was beyond most of us.

Welcome back

Two officers were back at work after being on long-term sick today. One had broken his thumb and the other had suffered a couple of puncture wounds after being stabbed with a biro while trying to take an inmate to the block. The knowledge that an officer is being taken to the outside hospital because of injuries they've sustained is one of the most worrying, unpleasant realities of the job – but it is a reality. Having people come back to work after recovering from their injuries was always good to see. Even if there must have been a part of them wondering, am I mad to return to this?

Bullying

Four inmates had been walking around the wing with an impressive array of injuries of late. We knew there had been some bullying going on but, when asked, the answer was usually the same – would you believe it, they'd all hurt themselves in accidents. Each one of them had been saying more or less the same thing: 'Just clumsy I guess, Guv.'

Another inmate discreetly handed me a note today that said that unless I moved him and his pad mate (cell mate) to the block, they would get done over. We tended to take these kinds of things seriously, especially with four walking wounded already on the wing, so we moved them to the Seg unit.

Never underestimate an inmate

The PWU was a small, secure independent unit, which housed three or four computers to be used by the inmates for education purposes. Someone was apparently using one of the computers to send and receive messages, which would require the use of a mobile phone. Was there a mobile on the unit and was a resourceful inmate or a member of staff responsible?

A lot of inmates are far cleverer and more skilled than people might imagine when they picture a prison – and we've had graduates, doctors and other educated types through the doors at Parkhurst. One of the men who escaped back in 1995 went to university. But even those at the other end of the academic spectrum often have street smarts and look at things in a different way to you or me. I quickly learnt not to underestimate an inmate.

Spinning the wing

We found several feet of home-made rope on the wing today. The immediate question here would always be: Is this just one piece of many or the whole thing? Either way, we conducted a big wing spin to find out. We found nothing.

Postal error

There had been a major, major cock-up in the mail delivery. An inmate with the exact same name as an officer was given the officer's mail. Anything remotely personal in an inmate's hands – an address or home phone number, even the officer's first name – would be compromising: any information gleaned could be used by inmates against the officer, even if it was just a bit of catcalling on the wing using the officer's first name. More worrying still would be the names of wives or children, or any other details about them. The number one governor and security were informed, and the inmate plus his cell mate were imme-diately scheduled to be transferred out.

The cycle to work scheme

I cycled in to work today and before I'd even had the chance to get changed, the alarm went off – and in the Seg unit, too, which was always serious. I raced to the Seg, where staff had been attacked by a particularly violent inmate. We had to do C & R to get the situation under control. This definitely isn't in the training manual, I thought as I struggled to get his arm in a lock while wearing my cycling gear.

Vicious circle

We had twenty-eight staff off sick today. We had around 220 uniformed staff, of which sixty-three didn't work on the wings. Take away those on various courses, those on annual leave . . . We were already running on MSL (Minimum Staffing Level), which was the absolute minimum amount of staff available to run a safe regime. Once the sickness levels get this high (more than 10 per cent of total staff), it becomes unsafe to run a normal day-to-day regime, so we have to keep inmates in their cells for longer. They don't like it. They get angry. They get pissed off. This puts even more pressure on us and some of us then end up going on the sick because of the stress. It's a vicious circle.

OD

I was doing nights, and it was the usual fun and games. An inmate rang his cell bell and said he was going to take thirty-five paracetamol. I told him in no uncertain terms that he wouldn't get hold of thirty-five paracetamol. He then showed me a handful of the things and proceeded to swallow them. There is a four-hour window before the medics can do anything regarding a paracetamol overdose; it has to be in the system for at least that time before tests are conducted. We knew that, and the inmate didn't, so there was no rush. I informed healthcare and he was eventually taken to the outside hospital.

A pain in the arse

It was a bit of a week for hospital visits. At 2.30 a.m., an inmate was taken to the outside hospital because he had taken an overdose and swallowed razor blades. It was a pain-in-the-arse escort for me at that time – though potentially a far more literal one for the razor-blade swallower.

Drugs

An inmate was strip-searched in a cell today, because he had plugged a quantity of heroin and then decided to fight the staff.

The problem with drugs was huge: crack cocaine, methadone, alcohol, cannabis, steroids and prescription drugs, often prescribed and issued in the prison.* Drugs for anything from pain relief to mental health, heart problems and epilepsy were sold, stolen or swapped. And then there was the trafficking.

The trouble with taking drugs inside is that they play havoc with an inmate's already fragile emotional state. To put it bluntly, it fucks them up. Is a drug like alcohol related to their crime? (For example, did they get drunk and kill someone?) Do they go violently off the rails when they take crack? Bullying, violence, theft, running up unpayable debts, addiction and mental health issues are just some of the consequences of drugs in the outside world, let alone prison, where they are amplified many times over. And those inmates deprived of the prescription drugs they genuinely need end up having to endure untold and possibly long-term harm, especially those with mental health issues. Drugs in prison are a nightmare for everyone.

---

* This was before spice started arriving on the wings.

What's in a name?

One inmate has tried to get a bit too clever for his own good. He officially changed his name to Sir, so that we would have to address him as 'Sir'. Officers, on the other hand, read it as Sear, and that is his name now.

Christmas Day

One thing that you never, ever do – well, two things, if you include trafficking – is go sick on Christmas Day. Staffing levels are always at a bare minimum and no one officially works their full shift – you usually only ever work three or four hours – and if everyone does just that little bit of the day, we can all have a fairly reasonable Christmas. This year, the wing's pisshead turned up to work still plastered. He was in no way fit for work, but it was Christmas Day and at least he'd turned up. He was shoved into an office to sleep it off. We covered his duties, annoyed with him, but he, like us, realised that if he wasn't 'on duty', we would all be working longer.

Christmas is a strange time in a prison. It's usually quiet and more relaxed, and we're always aware that it's a possible time for reflection, so rates of self-harming might go up. The inmates like to have a party if they think they can get away with it, so we usually do big hooch spins and try to spoil their fun.

CHAPTER 8

Governors

Within the prison there is the head of the prison, who is usually referred to as the number one governor, and then there are various other governors, each being the head of a department. The Seg unit, healthcare, race relations, reoffending – each have a governor. At one time we had one governor per wing, but now a governor will more likely have two or three wings or be responsible for a given area. We rarely see most of them and I've known officers who have been with us for several months ask, 'Who was that?' when the ghostly apparition of a governor makes a rare and all too brief appearance on the wing.

In my eyes, a good governor would be one who worked his way up and had spent years on the landing. One who knew the problems, shortcuts and reasons why things were done or not, and who had earnt the respect of his colleagues, if only because we are usually not the sort of people to give respect to just anyone. However, the rank of governor must always be respected – even if the person with that rank isn't respected.

The year 2010 would become a watermark year not only for the prison service, but also for the whole of British society. It was the year that a Conservative-led coalition government began to implement their austerity programme as part of their response to the 2008 financial crisis. Over the course of the next decade, funding for welfare and social services would be slashed, the police would have staff cuts in the tens of thousands and we would lose some 7000 prison officers thanks to budget cuts. By this time I was working on G wing – the 'foreign national' wing, which in theory housed those with limited English and no family members in the UK, but in reality was a title with no teeth, as inmates of any nationality were on every wing, and there were plenty of British inmates on G wing. It's fair to say that a sense of disillusionment in the job was becoming prominent among prison officers.

Jamaican language

I heard a story doing the rounds about a governor. A couple of days ago, he had turned up in G wing, apparently trying to impress the staff. After a few minutes spent looking around the wing, he went into the office, where he asked about the wing population, and when it was explained that there were a lot of East Europeans, South Americans and Jamaicans, he said he thought the information posters on the wing written in each language were a good idea and seemed to be informative, but why were there no posters in Jamaican? It was a tumbleweed moment. He continued digging his own hole and said that the next time he came on the wing he wanted to see the information posters up for the Jamaicans, too. It had to be pointed out to him that the 'Jamaican language' is English.

Please, sir, I want some more

Since about the mid 1990s, the decision had been taken to allow inmates to serve food instead of officers. It was a job most staff hated, so there were no complaints from us, though the inmates, of course, saw it as yet another opportunity ripe for exploitation.

I heard a story from another prison about an unexpected dinner guest at the hotplate one evening: a governor was present to observe the serving of the meal. As per usual the serving went without a hitch: over ninety inmates were fed in about twenty minutes, but a few hung around afterwards, which wasn't usual.

The servery workers, once they had completed serving the wing, served themselves, then started to dispose of the remaining food, which was prison service policy, and for good reason. The inmates milling around asked the servery workers if they could have the spare and were told, in no uncertain terms, no. They already knew the score. But the inmates are nothing if not adept at spotting weakness and any weakness will always be exploited.

Opportunistic and greedy, they approached the governor. They asked him – in fact, pleaded with him – to have the spare food. It seemed such a shame to waste it, they said. Prison service catering policy was such that it would never happen because it would open the flood gates to bullying, pilfering and God knows what else. The big boys would demand the surplus food, the weaker ones would be obliged to hand it over because failure to do so would in all likelihood result in a beating and the servery workers would either be exploited or start selling the spare food.

The prison officers knew the governor would say no, of course. Until, that is, he said, 'Yes.' He explained that the inmates did indeed have a point about wasting good food. In fact, from now on, rather than throw food away, they were to give out any spare food, because it was a crying shame to see good food wasted. 'Let them have seconds!' was the verdict.

They had nothing but problems after the governor's no doubt well-intentioned yet misguided intervention on the hotplate. Food was going missing, inmates were hanging around for seconds and whispering threats to the weaker inmates – 'You don't want that, do you?' – there was intimidation both from and towards servery workers, and some inmates were too scared even to go up to the hotplate. Today, the staff finally took matters into their own hands. They printed out the 'one man, one meal' policy, stuck it all over the wing and enforced it.

The night Snoopy staged a jail break

Late last night there was a very strange incident, so strange that it actually made the national newspapers. Our sister site, Albany, came under attack by Charlie Brown's pet dog, Snoopy.

It was a little before midnight, when the control room staff first became aware of something unusual happening at the main entrance to the prison on the surveillance cameras. It was a large white rabbit, or at least that's what the camera operator thought he saw, but he was on his second can of Red Bull so, just to be sure, he did a double take. After all, he reasoned, what would a six-foot white rabbit be doing out at that time of night?

He realised it wasn't a white rabbit – it was a Snoopy dog with an accomplice (his dog handler?) trying to gain entry to the prison. The alarm was tentatively raised and the O1 was called. The poor officer had to explain to the man in charge of the prison that he thought there was a man-sized Snoopy dog trying to break into Her Majesty's prison. It was never going to be an easy sell, and the O1 insisted on coming into the control room and checking the cameras himself.

The situation, however, quickly escalated. Snoopy and his pal were clearly frustrated at not being able to gain entry, so after smashing a glass panel near the front door, they headed towards the staff car park and started damaging the cars. They then went over to their own car and pulled out what appeared to be two shotguns from the boot, and pointed them at the prison. The situation was now serious and the police were called.

The sirens and blue lights arriving at the prison clearly spooked the pair and they did a runner. The prison cameras followed their every move and saw them ditch the shotguns while they ran along the outside perimeter wall. Now that they appeared to be unarmed, the police and prison staff gave chase to a giant Snoopy, like something out of the *Keystone Cops*.

They both soon ran out of steam and were apprehended, and it turned out that they had recently absconded from a mental institution in London. They thought that a family member had been incarcerated in the prison and they were hell-bent on freeing him. But while they were right about him being incarcerated, they had the wrong prison. When their weapons were recovered, they were thankfully found not to be shotguns but rather Super Soaker water guns.

Cowardice

On more than one occasion, I have raced to answer an alarm bell and arrived onto a wing only to be given directions by an officer who actually works on the wing.

'It's on the threes,' he might shout, and only when I'm halfway up the stairs do I realise that it's his wing and he should have been dealing with the situation, not directing the staff who have just run from the other side of the prison to attend.

Today, I was on the fives on B wing, when the radio bleep alert came across the net, followed by, '*Alarm bell, C wing, alarm bell, Charlie!*' I flew down the stairs and the officer on the ones held the gate open for me. The fact that he should have been halfway to the incident before I even reached the ones wasn't lost on me. Shaven-headed, thickset and with an impressive array of tattoos, this officer had arrived from another prison recently and was full of tales of fighting, take-outs, bend-ups and wrap-ups. He was, he informed us, a Seg unit screw through and through, and had once been involved in six take-outs in one day. He loved a scrap, and so the verbal diarrhoea went on. However, whenever there was an incident, he was always a little less than enthusiastic about showing us his legendary, deadly ninja-fighting skills.

Another occasion when this particular officer showed his reluctance to attend an alarm bell was when I was supervising the twenty-nine inmates who were on their exercise period. My radio sprang to life: '*Alarm bell, hospital. Alarm bell, hospital!*' I was supervising the exercise, a 'fixed post', which basically means you can't leave that post for any reason. I knew the staff would be tanking their way out of the wing, so to save them valuable time I got the gates open and ready.

Half a dozen officers came storming through, the reluctant warrior officer coincidently bringing up the rear. He shouted to me, 'You go, I've got these!' indicating that he was taking over the exercise supervision. I ran towards the hospital and had a glance towards the officer alongside me: he was laughing at the stupidity of it and I couldn't help but join in.

Occasionally, and it's happened half a dozen times that I know of, an officer or some other rank will receive an envelope containing nothing more than a single white feather. It's a tradition that apparently derives from cock fighting, which makes clear that his colleagues think him a coward. Personally, I can put up with a coward as long as I know he is one. I really don't want to be storming into a situation with an officer who has told me and anyone else who'll listen that he loves a scrap, only to turn round and find I'm on my own. If I know I'm with a coward I'll act accordingly.

The great phone hunt

Almost every prison in the country has a huge mobile phone problem. Prisons are awash with them, and they can be used to intimidate both witnesses and victims, conduct deals for drugs and even in escape attempts. They can be used to photograph the prison and staff, and they can be used to plan where to pick stuff up (usually drugs or more phones). Photographs can also be used to copy keys (which is just one reason why it's so important for an officer to keep his keys on him and out of sight) and threaten staff. And mobile phones offer the convicted criminal the opportunity to carry on with business as normal.

Today, however, the security department received delivery of an all-singing, all-dancing wonder gadget that would be a great weapon in the prison's fight against illegal mobile phones. This gadget was apparently able to locate a mobile phone's location to within a couple of feet. Trials commenced immediately, and early indications were promising. It was then decided to do a test run by getting someone to hide a phone and then use the gadget to find the thing. A member of the security team was instructed to throw an old, confiscated mobile phone over the prison wall from outside the prison, and then the search began.

After completing a circuit around the prison perimeter, the wonder gadget had failed to pick up any reading of the phone. The instruction manual was reread, batteries were checked and there was still nothing. The officer who had thrown the phone was asked for a rough location of the phone. Each section of the wall was allocated a number in the prison, should staff need to be directed to that particular area in an emergency, and the security officer gave them the wall number where the phone was. But there was still absolutely nothing.

After a couple of hours of fruitless searching, the security department decided to do things the old-fashioned way: on their hands and knees in the dirt, crawling along and fingertip searching the area. Still no sign of it. Finally, they gave up for the day.

The great cock-up

After yesterday's phone-hunting debacle, it was discovered that the officer who threw the phone over the wall had actually turned the phone off before throwing it and the wonder gadget would only detect a phone that was switched on.

Night terrors

As I arrived for my night shift, an ambulance was just pulling out. An inmate by the name of Zippy Hibbson was on board.

Old Zippy was well known to the staff and was called Zippy for a good reason: his party piece was to slice open his own stomach and remove bits of intestine. I first met him when his cell bell went off and, as he wasn't banged up and didn't need to ring the bell, I went to his cell to reset the bell and find out what his problem was. He was sitting on his bed holding something in both hands. The moment I entered his cell, he looked at me and said, 'Guv, I've done it again.' And done it he had. He was holding a handful of his own intestines still attached to his body.

He had done this form of self-harm so often that the scar on his stomach now looked like an actual zip. However, tonight he had done it once too often and needed to go to the local hospital. The hardened scar tissue was in such a poor state that they couldn't stitch poor Zippy together again and he was soon on his way to a specialist plastic surgery unit for reconstructive surgery.*

At a little after 2 a.m., a cell bell went off and on arriving at the cell, I saw that the inmate had apparently mummified himself in what must have been about a dozen toilet rolls. He was swaddled from head to foot. The cell was littered with what looked like a snowfall of torn-up paper. He had a lighter in his hand, which he was flicking on and off.

I called it in and tried to speak to him. He ignored me. Del turned up and tried the same. He got a 'Fuck off!'

---

* Poor Zippy would die of sepsis several months later.

and I got the fire hose. Del called for another officer and a healthcare worker to attend, and once they arrived, and with the fire hose ready, he cracked the door open.

Fortunately for us, the inmate dropped his lighter and broke down in tears. We slowly unwrapped him, opened an ACCT and put him on a 'constant watch', which meant moving him to a cell with a barred gate so he could be seen at all times.

2011

Another day in paradise

It was so busy today at the prison that I felt like I had run the equivalent of a half-marathon by the end of it. Five alarm bells went off, two of which were serious and involved fighting and assaults, and one officer got injured in the Seg unit. After unlock at 18.00, things seemed to have quietened down. Things got *too* quiet, in fact, which was never a good sign.

From our vantage point in the observation boxes on the end of each landing, with two officers in the one box on each landing, everything seemed normal, albeit without the usual verbal ranting and raving exchanged on the various landings. And then it happened. There had been an assault and someone was rather unceremoniously thrown down the stairs onto the landing below. The alarm was instantly hit and the staff appeared with the usual shouts to bang up the wing. The trouble, as always, was that even those who actually want to bang up and want absolutely nothing to do with whatever is happening won't, because they simply can't be seen to be compliant or willing to make the screws' lives easy. They drag their heels, put on a bit of a show for their peers and eventually go away.

Unfortunately for us, this particular night was a little different in that all the handles on the cells had been covered in excrement and many of the locks had been pencilled. The planning and organisation that went into doing this during association was actually rather impressive. Staff are usually observing things from one end of the landing, but the resourcefulness of an inmate can never be underestimated. It's surprisingly easy for inmates to jam the locks with a pencil, even while we're on the landing. A cell door opens into the cell, so they just open the door, jam the lock and walk back out onto the landing. We are usually totally oblivious until it's too late.

When this sort of thing happens, your senses go into overdrive. You watch and listen for any immediate threat, usually from above. Your sense of smell kicks in, on high alert for the fragrance of shit, fire, blood – even fear. You move differently, on the defensive, without even realising it.

The troops quickly arrived. Gloves were issued. At one time the dogs would have been brought in as a little canine encouragement, but we had lost our dog section by now and only had a couple of drugs dogs rather than the Alsatians. The medics tended to and removed the victim of the assault. We eventually cleared the landings, banged up all the inmates and accounted for each of them.

It turned out that the victim was someone who had not only run up a sizeable debt at his previous prison, but had also beaten the shit out of the brother of one of the inmates at Parkhurst. Though this had all happened several years ago, inmates have long, vindictive memories and a contract was put out for the debt. The person who fulfilled the contract was the ever-patient, revenge-seeking brother, who was more than happy to get even with the person who had beaten up his younger brother while getting paid for it – two birds, one stone. Why the locks and handles were shitted up and jammed, we never knew. Just to annoy us, most probably.

The element of surprise

Every so often, security would arrive very early in the morning, set up shop and search all the staff arriving for work. A simple enough and important job. However, the fact that the car park was unusually full at silly o'clock in the morning would warn everybody up to no good that the searches were in progress. If any staff were up to no good, they just had to work in pairs. One would go in and, if no searches were being conducted, he would just phone his partner in crime to let him know the coast was clear.

A couple of weeks ago, one of the security governors had given the night orderly officer an almighty rollicking for unlocking the prison several minutes early. So today, when the governor turned up with seventeen searching staff at the prison gates twenty minutes prior to the prison being unlocked, the night orderly officer informed him that he would have to wait until the official unlock time, as per his own recent order. This resulted in the farcical situation of the security staff hanging around outside the prison as the regular staff turned up for work. The element of surprise was most definitely lost.

Choose a secure password

The latest story doing the rounds was that a governor at another prison had lost the new password for one of the safes. Well, not lost, exactly. He had apparently changed the electronic password so that only he knew it, then written it down on a piece of paper, which he then put in a secure place: *the safe*. He couldn't remember what he had written, so the safe had to be cut open by a Home Office specialist at great cost, rendering it redundant as a safe but the perfect place for storing the tea and coffee.

Caught in the act

I was on the fours this afternoon, when an officer on the twos, who was doing LBBs (locks, bolts and bars, a daily check on the integrity of the windows, locks and bolts, basically making sure they haven't been tampered with) found two inmates *in flagrante delicto*. He placed them on report. The adjudication was the next day.

An innocent mistake

It was, or should have been, an open-and-shut case. They were, after all, caught bang at it. The evidence was heard: 'Sir, at the time, date and place stated, inmates A and B were caught naked and indulging in an illegal sex act, namely anal intercourse. Both were naked from the waist down, with inmate A's erect penis seemingly inserted into inmate B's anus.'

However, when the inmates were given the opportunity to put their case across, it transpired that the silly officer had got it all wrong. What the officer had actually witnessed was inmate A saving the life of inmate B, who was apparently choking to death. Fortunately for him, inmate A knew how to execute the Heimlich manoeuvre.

While admitting that his penis was indeed erect, inmate A maintained that he wasn't aroused. The adjudicating governor agreed that the officer had actually witnessed a life being saved thanks to the heroic efforts of the inmate administering the Heimlich manoeuvre. The nicking was consequently thrown out – no case to answer.

The wheelchair-pushing course

The prison was in the news this week because apparently an inspectorate team had come in and said that the place wasn't only rife with bullying, but, even worse, the staff wouldn't push inmates in wheelchairs around. They went on to say that prison officers wouldn't volunteer to do the wheelchair-pushing course. (Yes, there was actually a course to meet a certain proficiency.) It claimed that one inmate hadn't had a shower for a year and another for six months, and it was all because the prison officers refused to do the wheelchair-pushing course.

The truth, as ever, was a little different. No mention was made of the fact that the prison employed numerous healthcare staff. Nor that the prison was constantly being run on MSL, (Minimum Staffing Levels), and the clue is in the title. Only the bare minimum of staff were ever on duty and having spare staff to push inmates around would be an unbridled luxury only rarely available. In any case, the 'qualified' officer would have to be released from whatever duty they were currently performing to push an inmate around, so who would take over their duties? It's just not practical. An officer should be aware of his periphery. We need to know what's going on around us and the fact of the matter was that an officer with both hands on a wheelchair, concentrating on transporting an inmate, in a 'minimally staffed' prison, instantly became vulnerable.

Nicknames

Nicknames stick. Like the officer called Two Scoops who got his nickname because when he first started, he was, like the rest of us, put on the hotplate to serve meals. He was on mashed potato and should have given the inmates one scoop; instead, he gave two. A simple enough mistake that saw him spend the rest of his career in the service* being called Two Scoops.

Sinex was an irritating little squirt who got up everyone's nose. Chocolate was the name given to an officer who melted when things got a little heated. Another officer was called Two Shits. He was sort of proud of this name because he assumed he'd earnt it because he didn't give two shits. But he was actually given it because he was one of those annoying people who always claims to have gone one better than you: he had a blacker cat than your black cat; if you played football at the weekends, he had been a semi-pro some years ago; if you'd been in the army, he'd been in the special forces; if you caught a nine-pound fish, his tipped the scales at a little over ten; if you had one shit, he had two.

Another officer was called the Hooded Claw, because whenever he was detailed to work on a wing, he would cover his wrist with Tubigrip and state to all and sundry that he was unable to get involved in anything because of his injured wrist. He was also a chronic hypochondriac.

---

* Some thirty years.

Today, we took bets on how long it would take to convince him to go home sick – with a little encouragement from us, of course. When he arrived in the morning, he made a brew and an officer followed him into the tea room and said, 'Morning, Tone. You all right?'

A simple enough question for any normal person, but Tony had to answer, 'Yeah . . . why?'

'No, nothing. It's just that you look a bit peaky, mate.'

Like a well–choreographed dance, each of us then offered a similar observation throughout the morning. 'Blimey, Tone, you on the piss last night? You look fucking awful.' Then maybe a: 'You like look like shit, mate. Should you be at work?' And so it went on.

Within three hours the Hooded Claw was on his way home.

Patient or inmate?

An officer was assaulted in the Seg unit today. He was knocked out cold from a volley of punches, and the alarm was raised and the inmate restrained. When the medical staff arrived, a nurse got to work on tending to the officer, but was told in no uncertain terms by a governor to stop and tend to the inmate instead, whose hands and knuckles were sore and swollen after inflicting injury on the officer.

Bizarrely, this was in line with the rules. The NHS staff on-site were employed by the prison service to treat the inmates, not the staff. Thankfully, the healthcare staff always treated us when needed and she made sure the officer was OK. The inmate was removed in locks, with concern for his slightly swollen knuckles in short supply.

2012

Are you sitting comfortably?

When I turned up for work today, I was told there was a shortage of staff. An inmate had been blue lighted out to the hospital, with three officers in tow.

The unfortunate inmate had been cleaning his toilet and somehow got distracted, he claimed, when, with nature calling, he sat down on the toilet but had forgotten he'd left the toilet brush in the bowl, handle sticking up. The handle disappeared up his bum as he sat down. Unfortunately for him, the end of the handle was hooked and, try as he might, he was unable to dislodge the thing. Eventually, after much effort and with no little courage plucked up, he rang his emergency cell bell.

The officer who answered the call was hugely experienced and didn't bat an eyelid at the sight that greeted him. He asked all the right and relevant questions, then donned a pair of gloves and tried oh-so carefully to pull the brush out. Nothing. The bog brush was most definitely and firmly lodged.

The officer radioed for assistance, and it was decided that the best course of action was to get the inmate to the showers and lubricate the handle with copious amounts of soap. The medics were called and duly arrived, and they teased and tugged, pulled and prised, all to no avail. Once they realised that the end of the handle was hook-shaped, the decision was made to call the ambulance.

The prison grapevine went into overdrive and 'concerned' staff from all over the prison arrived to see for themselves – and, of course, offer help and advice, some of which was neither helpful nor advisable The inmate stood by his story that it had all been a terrible accident, a million-to-one chance. Officers listened politely, while desperately stifling sniggers.

The paramedics arrived and were quick to realise that hospital was the only safe place to extract the brush. It turned out to be so difficult that surgery was eventually decided upon, which would involve removing the handle through the stomach. The bristle end of the brush was cut off and drugs were administered to 'relax' the inmate. As a final effort to avoid surgery, one last go was attempted with industrial amounts of lube and with a little more teasing, tugging and gentle twisting, the thing was finally removed via the same route it had been inserted. Relief for the inmate at escaping surgery, though an awful lot of embarrassment seemed destined to come.*

Unofficial complaints procedure

This afternoon, an inmate came to the office complaining about having to be banged up for the umpteenth time when it was 'fuck all' to do with him. We politely reminded him that he was in prison and should a bang up be required, then a bang up will most certainly happen. Being a fairly new inmate, he was keen to impress his peers, so he wouldn't back down and gamely, if a little unwisely, pressed on. The more uninterested and bored with his moaning we became, the louder and more animated he got. It was just at the point of becoming tedious, when the inmate made the mistake of stepping forwards and into the office.

---

* He was, of course, called Basil after that.

Stuie was a softly spoken officer with one fatal flaw to his character: a fuse so short that had Usain Bolt himself lit the thing, he wouldn't have been able to run fast enough to get out of the way in time. And unfortunately for this inmate, Stuie's already limited patience was now used up and his short fuse had been ignited. Quick as a flash, Stuie was out of his chair and across the room to inform the inmate that it was now time to vacate the office.

This softly-softly approach unfortunately fell upon deaf ears – the inmate didn't move – so Stuie, now apoplectic with rage and with his face just inches away from the defiant inmate, told him in no uncertain terms: 'Fuck off out the office!'

When a six-foot plus, apoplectic Jock tells you to fuck off, fucking off would usually be the best course of action. The inmate now looked like he was about to crap himself and cry at the same time, and when he did manage to say something, it was a rather feeble and incoherent whine.

He was treated to another 'Get the fuck out the office!' from Stuie, but this time the inmate managed to pull himself together just long enough to say, 'I can't, Guv. You're standing on my flip-flop.'

Sure enough, Stuie was standing on the toe of his flip-flop, pinning the inmate to the spot.

Busted

I heard a story from another prison about a phone call the prison officers received from security to search four cells for hooch. They each paired up with a security officer and banged the wing up, which was greeted with a flurry of inmates hammering on doors and shouting threats and unsavoury comments about family members and wives in particular.

They proceeded to the fours to the first cell that they were to search (we always search cells in pairs), which was a double.* They gave the usual line of questioning: 'Is everything in here yours?'

They both nodded in unison.

'Have you got anything you shouldn't have?'

'No!' came the reply.

'Any legal paperwork in here?'

Again, 'No.'

One at a time, a strip-search was carried out and the inmates were then taken to the association room and locked in. It didn't take long before they found the hooch, four bottles of the stuff. The bottles were swollen, which confirmed to them that the fermentation process was well under way.

They finished the search and returned the inmates to their cell, asking each of them whose hooch it was. This was a formality, as usually one takes the blame, because there's no point in both of them getting into trouble. However, they both denied that it was theirs and both denied knowing anything about it, claiming that it must have been left there by the previous occupant. The prison officers took the hooch away and started on the relevant paperwork: cell-searching forms were completed, as was the 'nicking sheet'. They also printed off a copy of the Fab Check form, a tick-box form filled out prior to a cell

---

* There are criteria to meet to be able to share a cell. Lifers, for example, don't, likewise anyone with a history of violence against other inmates.

being occupied, which basically stated that a cell had been searched prior to occupation, that everything – taps, toilet light and so on – worked as it should and that the cell was now fit for occupation.

An open and shut case?

Both inmates had their adjudication with the governor the following day. They had both admitted when asked that everything in the cell was theirs and they had also signed the Fab Check form to this effect. It seemed to be, as the Americans would say, a slam-dunk case. *Wrong*! The governor couldn't decide who was responsible, so he found them both not guilty. The hooch was disposed of and the inmates were returned to their cell, and the officers felt like mugs.

PART III:

Outside Parkhurst – The Albany Years

CHAPTER 9

Morning, Guv

Starting again

I checked the detail when I arrived today and found I was down to work for a few weeks in Albany, the sister site of Parkhurst.★ Back in 2009, the two prisons, along with HMP Camp Hill in Newport, had been merged to form one institution called HMP Isle of Wight. I know at Parkhurst we weren't overly happy about the merger. Call it pride, but we felt that Parkhurst was its own place with its own identity and I gather a lot of people at Albany felt likewise about their prison. Camp Hill, which had endured a lot of bad press (the only kind of press prisons ever get) in recent years, officially closed just a couple of months before, in March 2013, as part of a cost-cutting drive, which saw a lot of jobs lost.

Albany was home to the sex offenders, necrophiliacs and baby killers. Ageing, has-been show-biz types, animal lovers, paedophiles, scumbags, pond life and an assortment of so-called VPs were held there. These prisoners had committed the most depraved acts, crimes that, in a couple of cases, I had never heard of and could scarcely imagine. Crimes that I thought would have been physically

---

★ Or so I thought – I'd actually spend the rest of my career in the service working here.

impossible. My first feelings were that this was going to be like working in a leper colony.

Built in the sixties, Albany was, to borrow Prince Charles's description of the proposed new National Gallery extension in 1984, a 'monstrous carbuncle'. It wasn't fit for purpose and was as close to being derelict as is possible without actually being condemned. The fabric of the place looked like a badly neglected inner-city council tower block. This was immediately apparent when I walked in, out of the pouring rain. There were buckets everywhere and bits of water-damaged plaster hanging off the walls, with puddles and wet footprints leading me down the corridor.

The one extremely tangible quality was the silence. I couldn't believe my ears. When you walked through the grounds at Parkhurst there was a constant cacophony of shouted threats, orders and instructions in a multitude of languages and accents, while improvised 'fishing' lines delivered snout and God knows what else through cell windows, and discarded rubbish, nicking sheets, newspapers, slightly soiled porn mags and, of course, the ubiquitous shit-parcels also came out. In a prison like Parkhurst, cell windows were so much more than a simple aperture.

Albany was a complete and utter contrast. You could actually hear birds singing in the prison grounds, staff whistling and chatting, key chains rattling, and doors and gates being opened and closed. There was even a little aviary, housing an array of exotic multicoloured birds, set in a well-maintained garden area. It was, I have to say, a shock to the system, but not as shocking as when an inmate actually said, 'Morning, Guv.'

'Fuck off, Guv,' I could understand. 'Morning, Guv,' was language from another world. I was now feeling a little unsettled. The transition from the Parkhurst way to the Albany way was going to be difficult.

I was used to dealing with inmates who wouldn't talk to or acknowledge you, but Albany's inmates were completely different. Talkative, chatty and polite (though most were odd-looking and strange), their courteousness, to this cynical old screw's instincts, appeared to be superficial, offering them the chance to creep, ingratiate, manipulate, worm and wheedle their way around staff of all ranks.

I didn't think I was easily shocked after over twenty years at Parkhurst, but when a bloke in pink shoes, a short skirt and badly applied make-up walked towards me and bade me 'good morning', well, I must admit, it did catch me off guard. The scene presented before me, I'm sorry to say, reminded me of the Kenny Everett character Cupid Stunt. I went home from today's shift more exhausted than any I'd done previously, thanks to a load of demanding and whinging inmates who, worst of all, loved to talk. Mainly about themselves.

The day I met a rock star

One of the more famous inmates – or at least famous to those of us brought up in the 1960s and 70s who tuned in to *Top of the Pops* – was a glam rock star who was now just another little old man who had been found guilty of paedophilia. As we called for exercise today, he shuffled his way towards me and, despite the fact that I knew exactly who he was, I asked him his name. He wasn't overly impressed. His reputation might have been shot to pieces, but his ego remained intact.

A prison song

Mr Former Glam Rock Star's ego took a further kicking today when he started singing on the landing. A man who had once held audiences in the palm of his hand was now told in no uncertain terms to 'Shut the fuck up, you muggy cunt!'

Telling tales

One of the most annoying things about Albany was the fact that the inmates were all grasses. In the main prison, if an inmate grassed, there was an extremely high price to pay. Mind you, if an inmate was seen talking to staff there was a price to pay. But in Albany the inmates would grass each other up about anything and everything, which had the unfortunate knock-on effect of generating paperwork that you had to follow up on. Because if you didn't, the inmates would grass you up.

I was working in the education department today. At Parkhurst, two officers see in and check the inmates: the inmate hands over his ID card and one officer confirms the inmate's ID while the other checks the list of names. Once happy, the inmate is allowed in. Albany was a little different: the inmate tells the officer his name and the wing he came from, and one officer just accepts what he has been told and allows the inmate to proceed. I must have looked a little confused (again), because the other officer told me that the inmates weren't prone to bullshitting or lying to staff; if one did give a false name, the one behind would grass him up. 'These types of inmates,' he explained, 'the VPs (vulnerable prisoners) are people-pleasers by nature.'

This certainly caught me off guard. It had been hammered into me at Parkhurst that inmates, if they decide to talk at all, will lie to you, fuck you about and make life thoroughly unpleasant. Had I turned into a cynical old man who thought he knew best?

I was even more confused when the inmates arrived and, when asked, they each told the officer their name, location and even the class they were attending. It was either a revelation or manipulation on an industrial scale. But when the numbers were reported to the control room and everything tallied, I was both impressed and relieved.

Trust

This trusting inmates and their word happened again on E wing. The custodial manager (CM), newly arrived on the wing, after having spent many years on a con-free diet, decided to keep his hand in and make his presence felt by helping us to unlock for labour. We were short-staffed (again), so we only unlocked the inmates who were due to go to work, leaving the rest banged up.

I got my list of names together and started work, but the CM in his naivety simply asked every inmate on his landing, trusting their answers and relying on their word, then couldn't understand why so many were out on the phones, in the showers, passing things on other landings. Being as short-staffed as we were meant that the difficult job became unnecessarily more difficult and confrontational, as we had to now chase up inmates to get them back behind their doors. Trusting inmates was something I could never get to grips with.

Self-diagnosis

Beeny was an inmate desperate to be removed from the wing because he claimed he had mental illness. But, like any other inmate on the wing, he was exactly that – any other inmate – and he was treated as such. We weren't geared towards splitting the wing population, though each inmate was different, with different needs. Very often, inmates have special needs and might well need extra monitoring, such as learning difficulties, language barriers, gender issues, psychiatric and/or discipline problems. The list goes on.

Apparently, Beeny had never been a discipline problem; he was, by all accounts, just a pain in the arse. He was constantly telling staff and anyone else who would listen that he was mentally ill and that he shouldn't be there. He should be in a special hospital, he said, because he was 'mad' – 'fucking mad', as he put it.

Today, he was being a bigger pain than normal, saying he could hear voices and that if he didn't see a nurse, something would happen – because, again, he was mad, he made it very clear. And so it went on. The staff listened intently, nodded and agreed with him that yes, something should be done and it wasn't right, the wing definitely wasn't the right place for him, basically repeating ad nauseam what they already said to him on a daily basis. He went away feeling a little reassured that the officers were on his side – or so the officers thought.

About an hour later, Beeny appeared at the office, his head and face smeared with blood. He said, 'See, I told you I was mad.' In his desperation to prove the severity of his madness, he had carved three letters into his forehead for all the world to see. There could be no doubting it now, they would have to send him out.

One of the officers then asked him why he written 'dam' on his head. He said, 'No, it says "mad", not "dam".'

Another officer was asked to confirm what was on Beeny's head. 'Looks like someone's cut "dam" on to your head.' Poor old Beeny, using a razor and mirror, hadn't allowed for the optical effect of mirror writing, which confirmed to all of us that he wasn't mad – he was just fucking stupid.

Accused

I knew this was going to be a difficult adjustment to life at Albany. I was called into the governor's office today, as a formal allegation had been made against me by an inmate. The governor explained that the allegation was serious. I had, according to the victim, 'subjected the inmate to torture', and not just the once but on three separate occasions.

What the fuck? was my first thought. The governor had the foresight to soften the blow by informing me that I wasn't the only officer accused of this heinous act; there were three of us. I wasn't sure if this made me feel better or not, but I was certainly confused. I had been involved in a few tussles that had resulted in inmates being removed to the Seg unit, under restraint (wrist locks), but it had all been done by the book, as far as I was aware. The Home Office-approved C & R techniques had been properly applied and while I was aware that I was far from as proficient as the Seg staff, I had a bit of experience behind me. Each removal had been supervised and the paperwork had been signed to say that there were no problems. All inmates are checked for injuries by the healthcare medics and there had been no concerns or issues with any of the removals for any of the staff involved. There had certainly been no mention of torture.

I racked my brains. I had never drawn my stave or hit an inmate, and I'd certainly never inflicted any form of unnecessary physical pain. I was at a loss.

The governor informed me that on three separate occasions I had made Prison National Offender Management Information System (PNOMIS) entries that referred to the inmate in the masculine. I had written 'him', 'his' and 'he', which was in complete violation of the inmate's human rights.

Now, I was really confused. According to his PNOMIS notes, the inmate's name was Philip, his gender was down as being male, he was born in 1967 and was sentenced seven years ago for the rape of a female. The fact that he was also in a male prison was a major clue regarding his gender.

The governor informed me that he/she had recently decided to become female and from the moment that decision had been made some nine weeks ago, he had become Philippa. Because I had been so cruel by referring to her, on more than one occasion, as a male, the inmate had felt violated and his/her human rights had been violated. Consequently, I was now in the shit and under investigation.

One of the other officers was under investigation because the same inmate had complained that the officer had refused to let her be served on the hotplate wearing a skirt and flip-flops. The governor backed the inmate, stating that any inmate on the Transgender Pathway programme, essentially a contract that confirms a male inmate wants to become female, was entitled to wear female clothing around the prison. The staff were pissed off, because we are obliged to enforce and strictly adhere to prison service dress code policy, which clearly states that shorts, vests and flip-flops are not to be worn when collecting meals from the hotplate. We could see that this was now opening Pandora's box: male inmates would have to abide by the policy, but the inmates who wore dresses were free to accessorise them with flip-flops, skirts, camisoles and make-up at the hotplate.

Now, I know I might sound a bit old-fashioned, but I don't have a problem in society with this kind of gender fluidity. I fully understand that some people of either sex suffer from gender dysphoria, and that it's becoming a more open and accepted part of life. What I do find incredibly suspicious, however, is when a convicted sex offender, who committed his crime as a male, suddenly wants to change his name and gender while inside prison.

The vast majority of inmates aren't stupid and they become adept at spotting a flaw in the system. And when the system is so obviously flawed, it's nothing more than just another gift, ready to be exploited. The inmates who say they want to change gender appreciate the fact that they can, according to prison service policy, alter and customise their prison-issue clothing, which used to be a nickable offence, as it was deemed to be damaging prison property. Likewise, they can have a shower in private; no such courtesy is afforded to the other inmates, straight or gay.

Conducting a search on a transgender inmate, whether they're genuine or not, becomes a nightmare. It requires four officers instead of the usual two: two female officers search the top half, then two male officers search the bottom half. Then you have the logistics involved. Finding two available male officers and two available female officers, if they do happen to be on duty, in a minimally staffed prison, who will have to be released from whatever job they are doing and replaced while the search is carried out, can be incredibly difficult, and the inmates know it.

Inmates who say they are changing gender can revel in a degree of privacy that includes staff having to knock on the cell door before entering or before using the observation panel. Basically, we now have to pre-warn inmates that we are about to catch them up to no good.

No actual hard and fast evidence regarding the inmate's gender transition is required. The only thing needed to make this apparent transition official is the inmate's word. The word of a convicted prisoner, no less.

Part-time pathway

We had an inmate on the wing who had applied and been accepted for the Transgender Pathway programme. He changed his name. He wore his floral print dress, ill-fitting syrup (wig) and make-up that looked as if he had applied it using his feet. He understood that he would be obliged to live life as a female for two years. He walked around the prison, attending work and the library as if he were a glamorous supermodel. He even wore female clothing while being escorted to the outside hospital, which was bloody embarrassing for the unfortunate staff escorting him, with kids, being kids, pointing and asking the obvious question: 'Mummy, why's that man wearing a dress?'

It was all going well until he had a visit from his family today. He didn't want them to see him dressed as a female, despite his commitment to living as a female. Now, call me a cynical old screw if you like, but surely you don't get to have an afternoon off from something you've made such a big and serious commitment to. But the governors didn't agree. He was allowed to attend his visit dressed as a male, confirming to us all, except the governors, who allowed this charade to happen, that he was just another inmate playing the system.

This was a world away from Parkhurst. I was so confused by it all that I paid a visit to the officer responsible for equality. They sort of helped, I think, by explaining that there was a world of difference between transgenders, trans-sexual, transvestite, transfluid, intersex and cross-dressers. Apparently, it was up to us, as individuals, to establish with the prisoner the degree of the expression of their gender identity – whatever that actually meant. And I thought it was our job to keep the prisoners locked up and safe, and maintain a degree of discipline.

2014

Man's best friend

Albany was a very confusing place. An inmate who had made a formal complaint about his magazine being with-held was informed today that, owing to the nature of his crime and his history of repeat offending for the same crime, he wouldn't be allowed this particular magazine in his possession. Apparently, it was related to his crime and was considered to be the inmate's equivalent of pornography; consequently, it would have to be placed in his stored prop (inmate's property that is stored in the reception area of the prison). The magazine in question was *Horse & Hound*.

Near-death experience

An inmate decided to set fire to his cell today. Despised by the other inmates, he had apparently run up a sizeable debt, so in desperation, he set fire to his cell with himself in it. It didn't take a genius to work out that he needed to get off the wing. Unfortunately for him, before the alarm was raised, the other inmates, to whom he was likely in debt, had got wind of what was going on. They barricaded his cell, silenced his cell bell (which is done from outside the cell) and pencilled his lock, making it difficult and time-consuming to gain access and rescue the idiot. He was eventually pulled out, but very nearly died.

Misters

I was in trouble again. I had started all my ACCT document entries with 'This inmate . . .': 'This inmate attended work', 'this inmate went out on exercise' and so on. Apparently, this was disrespectful. I was informed that the 'people in our care' were to be addressed as either 'men' or 'Mr'. I couldn't win and I couldn't keep up with this ever-changing bollocks. To me, an inmate was an inmate, plain and simple.*

---

* I never did get round to calling them Mr – nor did a lot of other experienced officers. Apparently it was something we were encouraged, but not obliged to do. It was, we were told, to break down barriers between staff and inmates. Call me old-fashioned, but I thought a barrier between officer and inmate was important.

UV protection

We were standing on the landing this morning, talking about the recent events at HMP Dartmoor. Apparently, the inmates had decided to hold a demonstration on the roof of the prison. The governors had, so we heard, leapt into action. They didn't appear to be concerned about the possibility of inmates damaging the fabric of the building, or the safety of staff potentially under fire from roof tiles and anything else the inmates might have to hand. No, the governors had more serious problems to deal with. It was a hot and sunny day, and of paramount importance was offering the inmates some suntan lotion. It was a duty of care, after all, and you can't be too careful where those harmful UV rays are concerned. The concerned onlooking staff were able to breathe a collective sigh of relief as they slowly roasted in riot gear.

This story made the national press, which just goes to show it doesn't always have to be something bad about prisons that makes the papers; it can be something farcical, too.

Oiling up

We were in the middle of another gloriously hot sunny spell. Hot spells can be a bit more unpleasant than usual in prison, as the inmates can get a bit smelly, grumpy and even more short-tempered in some cases, but they have their own desktop fans in their cells, so they don't roast once they're banged up.

O1 came onto the wing today with a carrier bag and looking a bit sheepish, which naturally piqued our interest. When we asked what was in the bag, he reluctantly said that he had been instructed to hand out bottles of suntan lotion to each wing. It would be our job to ask the inmates politely to apply Ambre Solaire before going outside, especially onto the exercise yard.

We thought he was winding us up, but we were told that it was no laughing matter. Some £200 had been taken out of petty cash and two members of staff despatched to buy the suntan lotion from Aldi. Our wing's photocopier had been out of action for nine days because we were waiting for an ink cartridge, but the suntan lotion had been purchased immediately.

To make matters worse, a governor on another wing was actually squirting the lotion onto each inmate's hand before they went out onto the exercise yard. We, of course, asked the obvious question: 'Where's our suntan lotion?' After all, we officers would be out on the exercise yard for far longer than the inmates. The silence by way of a reply said it all.

Favourite pastimes

The head of the mental health team arrived on the wing today and asked if he could speak to an inmate by the name of Maurice, a prolific sex offender and very real threat to females, with a history of assaulting staff of either sex. We explained that he was banged up at the moment, so I would have to go and unlock him and escort him down. The head of the mental health team said that he only needed a quick word and would happily see him in his cell.

I escorted him to the cell and, as usual, had a quick look through the observation hole prior to unlocking. The inmate was busy – stark bollock naked and kneeling on his bed, vigorously wanking onto his dinner plate. This was an inmate who took obvious pride in his work and he certainly wasn't going to be put off his stroke simply because a screw had looked through his observation hole. He looked straight at me and just carried on. I told the head of the mental health team that the inmate had his hands full at that particular moment and would he mind popping back later?

Ask a stupid question

Walter, one of the creepier old paedophiles on the wing (everything's relative, after all), asked if he could have a quiet word. These quiet words nearly always ended up with me having to do a shedload of paperwork, so I only reluctantly said yes and took him to the office.

'Mr B,' he said, 'a friend of mine has had sex with a dog and thinks he might have got it pregnant.'

My colleagues all suddenly appeared to be engrossed in paperwork. The only thing I could think by way of reply was to ask him what sort of dog it was. 'A dachshund,' came the reply. I told him that I didn't think he should worry.

'Thank you for your help, Mr B. He is really worried.'

The moment he left the office, the place erupted. Had he been put up to it? Was it all a joke at my expense? Unfortunately for the dachshund, it became clear that he was very much serious.

Wake up!

This morning, an inmate came to the office and said, 'Guv, I think you'd better have a look in cell one. He doesn't look right.' We went to the cell and checked on the inmate, who was sleeping soundly and snoring loudly, despite it being a little after 10 a.m.

The inmate, who had only arrived on the wing four days previously, was a big old unit. He weighed in at about 18 or 19 stone and certainly appeared to enjoy his food – even prison food. So when he didn't turn up for his lunchtime meal, which was served at eleven thirty-ish, staff became more than a little concerned. His cell was checked and he was still sleeping and snoring, but at a little before midday it was decided to wake him.

This wasn't easy. It never is. Softly-softly is my preferred approach; you know what they say about waking sleeping giants. I would usually have my foot behind the door and open with a, 'Jones, are you awake?' Then I'd shoot the bolt so the door couldn't be shut with me inside and make some noise before trying some repeated, louder variations on, 'Jones, are you awake?' Only once that failed would I attempt making physical contact, with a tentative touch on the shoulder, while being very much on high alert. And if that didn't work, well . . .

In the end, we had to inform the healthcare team that we had a rather large, somewhat corpulent inmate who wouldn't wake up despite numerous attempts. A couple of nurses turned up and, as the nurses were attending to the seemingly comatose inmate, the escorting officer spotted a note on the table. It appeared to be a suicide note, full of self-loathing and disgust. There was also a comprehensive list of the pills he had taken.

The nurses went into overdrive and asked for an ambulance to be called immediately. When the paramedics turned up, they removed his shirt and it was like a scene from *The Girl with the Dragon Tattoo*. In big, bold letters on his chest and torso were the words 'do not resucitate' along with 'paedophile', 'shit bag', 'dirty bastard', 'beast' and a few other self-deprecating – though accurate – notes to self. The paramedics immediately took him to the nearby A & E department, but not before telling the officers that they had in all probability saved his life.

Unfortunately, the governors saw it differently. Rather than praise the officers' efforts (as the paramedics had), the governors decided to initiate an investigation into lack of welfare.

The welfare policy

An instruction from the governor was given to all officers that we were to carry out 'welfare checks'. These were extremely important and would be conducted on each and every inmate the moment we unlocked. No one had heard of these 'welfare checks' before, including staff with over thirty years' service, as well as SOs and POs. We asked for a copy of the policy so we knew how to proceed.

The governor instructed another, lesser governor to come up with a 'welfare policy', but he was on leave, so implementing the extremely important 'welfare policy' could now wait until he got back.

CHAPTER 10

The Fire

2015

Arson

I was in the wing office, sorting out my annual leave and waiting to be relieved by the nightman. We got thirty-five days off a year, dependent on length of service, and we were also able to carry over seventy hours, which in an understaffed prison was easy to accrue. We were detailed five days of winter leave, five days autumn and ten days summer, and the rest could be taken on an ad hoc basis. I was grateful for a little peace and quiet to sort this particular bit of paperwork.

I was suddenly and rather rudely interrupted by the radio blaring out a bleep alert. O1 had just put out an urgent message to the control room, informing them that he 'had to get a team together'. Apparently, an inmate on A wing had refused to bang up. It was nearly the end of my shift and I just wanted to go home, so I rather reluctantly informed the control room that I was on my way. I knew that getting into C & R kit and the inevitable shedload of paperwork would put paid to any chance of getting off home on time.

I went to the wing next door to tell the officer that I was on my way to get kitted up and asked if she could keep an eye on my wing. Looking up from the computer screen, she asked, 'Why, what's happening?' She'd missed the urgent message because she was busy working on her *Candy Crush* score.

My radio suddenly transmitted another urgent message, again from O1, this time stating in no uncertain terms that he now needed the fire brigade. Things were now hotting up.★ I made my way to the C & R kit storage room, to be met by two staff trying to break into the locker because no one knew where the key was. I grabbed one of the two helmets and reported to O1, who said the inmate who refused to bang up was on the threes and had now started a fire on the landing using bedding, rubbish bins and anything that would ignite. However, there was one big problem: we couldn't get onto the landing.

Albany has a strange, somewhat antiquated system called 'Night San'. This 'Night Sanitation' system was put in place because the 1960s-built cells were unable to facilitate the necessary plumbing required to bring it up to date. As the law required each inmate to have access to a khazi, a computerised unlocking system was in place to allow one inmate at a time to leave their cell for seven minutes to use the toilet.

Each landing was secured and locked off by a Lima door, which confined the inmates to their own landing and was electronically locked; it could now only be opened from the control room. Once the inmate shut his cell door (which could only be done from inside the cell), the next inmate could come out. However, the inmate who set the landing alight refused to go behind his door and when we asked the control room to open the Lima door, it wouldn't

---

★ Sorry about that.

open. Something was wrong with it. We couldn't access the landing and deal with the fire or the inmate. There should have been an override system, but this was either not working, or there was an unqualified operator, which meant that we were reduced to little more than impotent spectators watching the pyrotechnic carnage unfold.

I made my way up to the threes and stood on the stairs behind Mark, a big, burly old-school screw who was handy in a scrap.* Our batons racked and ready, we were focused and all set to go in. The inmate was apparently suicidal, tooled up and desperate. Fat, angry and possibly high as a kite, he had nothing to lose and was going out in a blaze of glory. We knew we were going to have a fight on our hands. Well, we *would* have a fight if we could get on the frigging landing.

As the minutes ticked by, my nerves were becoming frayed. My helmet fogged up and the landing before us disappeared behind a veil of dense smoke. I removed my now useless, fogged-up and slightly oversized helmet, which was more hindrance than help. In these situations, I'm fine when the action is spontaneous and there's no time to think. It's the hanging around that's the killer. Confidence can wain and doubt creeps in.

More staff arrived as we continued to wait, fidgeting anxiously and just desperate to get on with it. And then someone noticed that the fours were on fire. The heat was so intense that it had actually ignited the landing above. With two landings now on fire, a total of forty-eight inmates were in immediate and serious danger. All we

---

* I learnt a long time ago that when the shit hit the fan, get behind the big bloke.

could do was just watch. Why the hell couldn't the doors be opened? Had the fire somehow damaged the electrics?

Was it operator error? This wouldn't have surprised anyone, as the prison had a knack of just filling the gaps. Staff shortages often meant people who hadn't been trained in certain aspects of a particular job would sometimes be put in a position where they had to fumble around and hope they got away with it. Nine times out of ten, you could just about wing it. But now, lives were on the line and we hoped that the inability to open the doors was down to fire damage rather than some poor sod without any training fumbling around with the computerised Night San system. I could imagine them being told exactly what I had on my very first shift, when I asked what the role of Juliet 6 was: 'You'll find out.'

At Parkhurst, fires, and cell fires in particular, were a regular occurrence. Here, they were a bit of a rarity, which, coupled with some inexperienced officers, had the obvious potential for disaster. Sure enough, when I looked up to the staff trying to get on the now flaming landing above us, a set of keys came hurtling past me and landed on the ones. Keys should never, *ever* be detached from the officer; keys, like radios, must be attached to the officer at all times. The nervous – frankly frightened – officer on the fours had somehow unclipped and dropped his keys.

The *Candy Crush*-playing officer then arrived and had the foresight to grab one of the official Home Office-endorsed flame-retardant smoke hoods, issued for the sole purpose of quickly snatching someone and pulling them to safety from a flaming cell. We were obliged to do an annual refresher course, of course. However, the moment she put her hood on, her face disappeared behind a veil of fog and she discarded it within seconds.

I was just pondering the whole farcical situation, which would have been funny were it not so fucking dangerous, when the cavalry finally arrived. The fire brigade were kitted out in no doubt the latest, most technically advanced flameproof, fire-retardant clothing, fog-free helmets and breathing apparatus that made me feel like I was standing next to Darth Vader. We, on the other hand, were wearing nothing but our uniform, white shirts and black trousers. Our confidence wasn't helped when the fireman in charge looked at the prison-issue flame-retardant smoke hoods and said, 'I don't know why you've got them. I wouldn't let my lads watch a bonfire in one of those.'

The dilemma now was who goes in first. Do the fire brigade go in first to fight the fire and make it safe for us, or do we go in first to deal with the inmate and make it safe for them? Though it was rendered moot by the fact that we couldn't get on the bleedin' landing. The fire brigade were as frustrated as we were, but the difference was that we looked at best unprofessional, at worst a bunch of incompetent clowns.

Some of us had tried to break through the toughened Perspex of the door with our extendable batons, but the fire brigade at least had in their possession the right tools for the job – or at least we hoped they did. First, they sent for an axe, which just bounced off the super-tough Perspex. Then they sent for a hooked spike, which they intended to use to pierce a hole in the Perspex and get a fire hose nozzle through so they could at least start to douse the fire.

The fire brigade got to work and were making some progress with forming a hole in the Perspex when, finally, we were informed that the Lima door could be opened and we now had access to the landings. It was a relief to finally be doing something other than waiting. We tentatively opened the door, while shouting out to the inmate. The smoke was blackish-grey and thick. Every intake of breath tasted foul and horribly noxious. We had little choice but to drop to the floor, which then left us extremely vulnerable to attack.

The only one of our five senses we could rely on was touch, so we crawled and groped our way to the arsonist's cell. Meanwhile, the fire brigade made their way to the source of the fire. It was a calculated gamble: we hoped the inmate was in his cell and not waiting in ambush for either the firemen or us.

Finally, we made it to the inmate's smoke-filled cell. We groped our way around and broke the cell windows in a desperate attempt to clear some smoke and get some air. We were struggling to breathe, so this needed to be quick. The trouble was, the inmate had tied a ligature around his neck and attached it to the window. We needed to cut him down and administer first aid. I handed my 'fish' knife to an officer, who managed to cut him down, then we had to drag this floppy and seemingly lifeless hulk out of there.

With our heart rates through the roof and the acrid smoke filling our lungs, the last thing we needed was a sweaty, slippery and obese dead weight. But through a combination of rather unceremonious dragging, pushing and heaving through the foul smoke, we finally got him off the landing.

We all slumped to the floor in a heap once we got to safety, sweating, coughing and spluttering, but thankfully each of us was in one piece. First aid was attempted on the inmate and he was handcuffed, just in case. Within minutes, he was taken to the Seg unit, where he finally came round. After various checks, the medics decided it wasn't necessary to send him to the outside hospital, so the cuffs could be removed.

Unfortunately, the CM didn't have the cuff keys on him. Phone calls were made and radio transmissions put out, but the cuff keys couldn't be found. The fireman in charge arrived to inform us that the damping down was now finally complete and his crew would be standing down. The CM, with self-preservation at the forefront of his mind after losing – or should I say misplacing – the cuff keys, then had one of those light-bulb moments: he asked the fireman if they had a set of bolt croppers they could use to cut through the handcuffs. They were happy to oblige – though I don't think it added anything to the air of professionalism we'd presented to the fire service.

While the utter arsehole of an arsonist was being secured and treated, the rest of the wing's inmates were being evacuated. Seven were taken out to hospital for immediate treatment owing to smoke inhalation and eighty-two inmates were in the gym. No one seemed to be taking a roll check, which was pointed out to the CM, who then asked an OSG to go round and count them, and get the names of the thoroughly pissed-off and frightened inmates.

Some staff were now coming in from home to take over. One of the managers arrived and walked straight past the three of us officers who were receiving oxygen and treatment from the fire service and immediately made his way over to an inmate being treated by one of the HCC nurses to see how he was. The three of us were taken to the outside hospital.

It wasn't reassuring that of the three services involved – the fire service, the National Health Service and the prison service – the one that seemed to show the least concern for the three prison officers who went out to A & E was the prison service.

The next day

I had a rest day anyway today, so I spent most of it coughing and wheezing after leaving the hospital. The fire had been declared a major incident, as we found out when we went to our local hospital, who were geared up and ready to receive a load of casualties – but only seven inmates went out.

Perks of the job

I was given £200 worth of shopping vouchers for my part in the fire, which was sort of a nice gesture but for two things: one, I hate shopping, and two, we lived on the Isle of Wight and most of the vouchers were only good for shops that we didn't have on the island.

It was decided that owing to the Night Sanitisation system being so unreliable and antiquated, a repeat fire couldn't be risked, so the decision was made today that any inmate with arson on his record wouldn't be housed at Albany.

The bigger picture

We came across an inmate today who had arson on his record. We confirmed this by checking his PNOMIS records and, as his personal officer, I asked him about it. He was quite open – blasé, even – stating that his pad mate* had pissed him off, so he'd started a fire in the cell while his pad mate was asleep. We contacted one of the managers and informed him that this inmate couldn't now be located on the wing, as he had arson on his record. The manager informed us that he would look into it and get back to us.

As good as his word, within a couple hours he got back to us. He confirmed that the inmate had indeed started a fire in a cell while it was occupied, but that it was some nine months ago and it didn't necessarily make him an arsonist. We checked again, but the manager would have none of it, stating that the inmate would remain on the wing. He then went on to explain that because he had only started a fire, he was actually just a 'fire starter', which didn't necessarily make him an arsonist. Perhaps it was another one of those 'bigger picture' things management kept telling me about that I wasn't privy to, but I still couldn't for the life of me work out what the difference was.

Each inmate has his own personal officer, who is responsible for doing monthly reports, such as PNOMIS entries, which are basically a summary of how the inmate has been over the last month: are there any changes, problems, concerns and the like? The personal officer is supposed to be the first port of call for the inmate. However, if the inmate and officer don't see eye to eye, or worse, the officer dares to tell the inmate something that they don't want to hear and have the audacity to use the dreaded 'no' word, the inmate in all likelihood simply won't bother talking to or asking the officer for anything, or will even ask to move cells just to get a different personal officer.

---

* Cell mate.

I've known inmates who, unhappy with their personal officer, have asked to change cells just so they can have a new one. At one point, inter-wing cell moves would never happen unless it was for operational reasons, but now they seem able to move to be near that very special friend, or for a better outside view, or to be nearer the phones or showers. Some inmates request multiple moves. And we allow it. Once again, the inmates dictate to us.

Procrastinating

Today, we had a situation with an inmate who was informed that he was to be transferred out. He went fucking ballistic, which was a little strange given that he hated the place and wanted out. He was told to pack his kit and get ready to be transferred out. Initially, it all went well – or at least it appeared to. The inmate packed his kit (this is usually a ploy, when inmates plan to end up down the block in the Seg unit), then came down onto the ones to inform us that there was 'no fucking way' he was moving and if we wanted him moved, then we would have to move him. He then walked to the association area and proceeded to smash the place up: dustbins and pool balls were thrown, pool cues were launched like javelins at the windows, and the flat-screen television was removed from the wall and smashed. He was, it would be fair to say, not a happy bunny.

The alarm was raised and the new O1 arrived. The four officers present informed him that we were happy to drop the inmate (physically restrain him and get him down on the Seg unit). O1 was a stickler for detail and said that we had to get kitted up. The kit store had been moved recently – to where, we had no idea. And nor did O1, as it turned out.

In the meantime, the inmate was causing more damage. We again offered to drop him and again O1 refused, quoting health and safety and saying we needed to be kitted up, as it would be deemed to be a 'planned removal'.*

An SO eventually arrived, who was a C & R instructor. He got a C & R 3 team together,† and after kitting up, they were briefed before quickly removing the inmate and relocating him on the Seg unit. The whole thing had taken approximately two hours and in that time, a shedload of damage had been done.

Entrapment

Covert testing was a cost-cutting, labour-saving approach to prison security. It was basically a form of entrapment: someone from security would leave a gate open and then watch to see if the next officer through the gate would report it. Other common practices by the security department involved things like placing a picture in an empty cell depicting a four-inch black dot, which was supposed to represent a hole in the wall. To anyone else it was a picture of a black dot.

A container of hooch was found in a photocopier this afternoon. It would have been funny had it not been so stupid. Any liquid in an electrical appliance is obviously dangerous, but alcoholic fermentation in the warm confines

---

* A planned removal is one that is extremely clinical and organised, during which officers must be suitably kitted up; a 'spontaneous removal' is an instant reaction and can't be planned.
† C & R 3 officers have done 'advanced C&R' and have their own kit to hand.

of a photocopier? Any self-respecting hooch brewer knows to release the pressure every so often, lest the thing explodes. The hooch was found in one of the large commercial photocopiers in the admin block, which was a con-free, secure area. Sellotaped to its side was a piece of A4 paper that read: 'This is a covert test, please report this find.'

2016

Prison-service technology

The prison service decided to get all twenty-first century. Ever since time immemorial we had collected our own issued set of keys from the gate by simply handing in our individual numbered 'tally' – a small brass disc engraved with an officer's personal key number – but now it had been decided that this was somewhat antiquated. A modern system allowing us to 'draw' any set of keys from a key safe using the latest fingerprint recognition system was introduced. Like so many of these things, it was a great idea on paper, but the reality was that it could be a temperamental pain in the arse. The technology often wouldn't recognise your fingerprint, which meant we were left unable to withdraw keys or return them. Not being allowed to get a set when you were going into work wasn't too bad, but it was a pain when you just wanted to go home and it wouldn't let you.

The Avon catalogue

As usual, we were sitting in the office filling out reams of paperwork – signing the usual things that needed signing and then signing to say we had signed the things that required a signature – when one of the civilian admin staff came in asking whether the inmate responsible for the Avon catalogues (yes, we had an Avon catalogue rep) had handed them out. I replied that yes, he had indeed handed out the Avon catalogues. The admin clerk was visibly relieved, and explained that the governor was on her case because one of the inmates had run out of foundation and refused to go to work without it. He absolutely couldn't attend the workshop without his make-up on and had the catalogues not been handed out, the admin clerk had been instructed to go into town and buy the inmate's foundation. The NEPO beside me, fresh to the gritty realities of life inside one of Her Majesty's prisons, couldn't believe what she was hearing.

Nostalgia

My job this afternoon was to supervise the Real Voices meeting. This was an inmate-led monthly meeting for those inmates who had chosen an alternative lifestyle but which felt like nothing more than a moan for the gay, transgender, transvestite, transsexual, bisexual, bi-curious inmates, many of them sex offenders and serving time for the vilest of crimes. Every size, shape, colour, creed, sexual orientation and religion seemed to be catered for among the inmates present. While they sorted out the seating arrangements and decided who took the minutes, I reported my numbers to the control room and found a place to sit in the corner, out of the way. This was going to be a long hour.

A middle-aged man wearing a short black dress and sporting a matching five o'clock shadow kicked off proceedings: 'Hello, my name's Philippa.' Each of the other twenty-three inmates present then introduced themselves before it was straight down to business. The first thing on the agenda was condoms and lube. Though the prison's HCC supplied both, the inmates wondered if they would be allowed to have flavoured condoms and if so, which flavour should they request. They couldn't agree and decided to raise the subject at the next meeting.

The conversation continued, moving quickly from one topic to the next. One minute the talk was of the perils of gay sex in public toilets – followed by heady reminiscences of the sexual services they offered for money, and the close shaves and bad times they'd endured – the next it was Avon catalogues, make-up tips and the best way to pad a bra. One tip was to use the caps of toothpaste tubes to make more prominent-looking nipples.

It felt like a gradual, creeping death as the hour ticked by slowly. I had thoughts of becoming a deckchair attendant on one of the local beaches. What a lovely stress-free job that would be.

And then, of all things, I found myself pining for Parkhurst. The old, forbidding place with its cacophonous din, its inmates who would as soon spit on you as say good morning, the sense of impending danger every time you opened an observation flap.

Had twenty plus years in the old place institutionalised me? It had certainly got under my skin, and the work at Albany just didn't compare.

How I longed to work with terrorists, serial killers or armed robbers once again, I thought as one of the Real Voices inmates pointed out to another that he had a ladder in his tights.

CHAPTER 11

Appeasement Policy

By 2017, the full impact of the country's austerity measures were being felt. The proliferation of the drug spice in the prison and the new, softer approach to inmates, which asked us to treat them more as people in our care rather than the convicted criminals they were, made a difficult and dangerous job more difficult, dangerous and frustrating than ever before.

Spice

I arrived for work this morning to learn that two of the night staff, O1 and an officer, had been rushed to hospital after inadvertently inhaling spice, which a violent inmate had been smoking. This nasty synthetic cannabinoid, labelled 'the zombie drug' by the media, is a far more potent drug than cannabis. While it shares some of that drug's high, it has some horrendous side-effects: vomiting, seizures, psychosis, aggression, confusion, extreme anxiety and hallucinations, to name just a few. It's an awful substance and, unfortunately, like every other prison in the country, spice had somehow flooded this prison, giving the inmates and staff some new and very real problems.

We attended the morning briefing, same as every day, to bring us up to speed about anything that happened overnight or might happen during that particular day. The governor informed us that the recesses had been

213

deliberately blocked with blue roll (like kitchen roll – it's everywhere in prison) and T-shirts last night and works had been called out to fix it. And also there would be a generator test at 15.00, for which we were to make sure we logged off any computers. We were then reminded that the prisoners were to be respectfully addressed as 'Mr' or as 'men', not inmates, prisoners, cons, lags or felons. The meeting finished with the usual, 'Are there any questions?'

A couple of hands went up. One of the officers asked about the well-being of the two staff who had been taken out by emergency ambulance to A & E after inhaling spice while dealing with the violent inmate. A blocked recess and a generator test were deemed important enough to get a mention, but apparently not the seriously ill, blue-lighted staff. Typical!

What made the whole spice thing worse was the fact that on the wings we all knew there was spice on the landings. We knew it was being smoked. Just a couple of weeks earlier, we had asked the DST (Dedicated Search Team) to come over and search the areas where we thought the spice was. Unfortunately for us, they couldn't come over 'because there wasn't enough evidence'. An email was then sent asking what evidence they needed in order to come over and search for spice. The reply was: spice.

If we could find some actual spice, they would then have enough evidence to come over and search for spice. A week after this debacle, and with the problem escalating, we asked for the prison's one and only specialist drugs dog to come over and help us to find it.* Unfortunately for us, it wasn't

---

* Back in the day, both Albany and Parkhurst had dogs sections, with kennels and numerous dogs; by the time I left there was just one dog for both prisons.

possible on that particular week because the dog handler was on leave, so how about the following week? But that wasn't possible either, because the *dog* would be on leave then.

Spice was a huge problem on the wing and it had severe knock-on effects. Volatile and dangerous inmates would become deranged and (even more) violent on the drug, which led to an escalation in violent incidents between inmates and, more importantly, against staff. A high-as-a-kite inmate in a spice-fuelled psychotic fury takes some stopping, trust me. And this incident that saw staff taken to hospital after inhaling it wasn't an isolated event. On another occasion, an inmate threw a load of spice into the office and several officers went to A & E after overdosing. The office had to be cleaned by specialists to remove all traces of the drug.

With the staffing levels at an all-time low – sickness was through the roof, TOIL was sky-high* – we had no choice but to keep inmates behind their doors for longer throughout the day. Association times were routinely cancelled, and inmates couldn't make phone calls and missed their gym sessions. This, of course, led to the inmates getting gradually more and more pissed off, and that anger would eventually be vented.

I hesitate to use the term war zone, because I've worked with people who've been in war zones, but the combination of spice and the lack of staff, and the resultant violence, were making the wings bloody dangerous places to be. It all came to a head, which resulted in a decision being made nationally at the end of last year (2016) that all staff

---

* I had 246 hours owing to me when I left the service and yet I never volunteered to work extra hours; they just accumulated, having to work through lunch times, tea time and staying behind at the end of shifts.

should retreat to a place of safety if governors tried to enforce unsafe working practices. Put simply, the workplace environment was now just too bloody dangerous.

As prison officers, we are generally a pragmatic bunch. Although I personally was not put in the position of having to 'withdraw' to a place of safety, I know it would have hurt, and hurt a lot. Call it pride, professionalism or stupidity, but the fact that we were advised to withdraw went against the grain. However, the fact of the matter is that an employer has an obligation to ensure the health and safety of their employees, and not place them in harm's way unnecessarily. Employers are obliged to ensure that employees are as safe as is 'reasonably practicable'. It's the law.

Those working at sea wouldn't be allowed to set sail in an unseaworthy vessel, firemen wouldn't enter a building deemed to be dangerous, the ambulance paramedic would wait for the police before entering a property or area deemed hazardous. Even the police would wait for backup should the situation require it. And yet prison officers were ordered, cajoled, coaxed and threatened with legal action to return to work in what had been decided was a 'dangerous environment'. Our local Prison Officers Association (POA) rep was even threatened with arrest.

The statistics were there to back us up. A 31 per cent rise in total assaults in prisons was reported in the year ending September 2016 compared to the previous year, which included a *40 per cent increase in assaults on staff.*★

★ Safety in Custody Statistics Bulletin, England and Wales. Ministry of Justice. September 2016 https://assets.publishing.service. gov.uk/government/uploads/system/uploads/attachment_data/ file/595797/safety-in-custody-quarterly-bulletin.pdf

The Ministry of Justice even came clean about the reasons, citing 'illicit psychoactive drugs' (spice), 'an increase in gang culture' and, crucially, 'staff reductions'. We had fewer staff than ever and yet more assaults on staff than ever before.

Rights and privileges

An inmate threatened an officer yesterday and attempted to ambush him. This particular inmate was as unpleasant as they come. He had only recently had nine years added to his sentence for attacking an officer so badly that the injuries sustained were life-changing, resulting in the officer having to leave the prison service.

This threat to our officer was menacing and sincere, and was backed up by the fact that he'd tried to get the officer on his own on three or four occasions. Though he had only recently arrived at the prison, he was keen to make a name for himself and show his peers that he was the real deal: a proper 'hardman'.

Once the potential attack had been thwarted, the relevant paperwork was submitted, PNOMIS entries made and reports written, and the inmate was placed on report. The inmate refused to attend today's adjudication and the recommendation was made to place him on the 'Basic Regime'.

The recommendation was ignored, seemingly because placing the inmate on the 'Basic Regime' would only upset him. He would also probably be angry and annoyed with the officer, the very same officer who he'd threatened to assault. Consequently, the inmate would remain on the wing with the officer he had made very real threats against.

The managers now seemed so determined to give prisoners everything they wanted that they had even made 'tailored regimes'. Years ago, everything was black and white, a simple yes or no. It was a screw-proof system. An inmate would either be on Basic, Standard or Enhanced regime. There were few enhanced prisoners, because getting onto the enhanced regime was deliberately made difficult. An inmate would have to work hard over a period of time, be patient and pull out all the stops. Just as in the real world, he would have to work hard for the benefits and rewards.

It seemed now that we had given the inmate everything, and given it to him immediately, that as long as he was prepared to plod along, he could keep it. The trouble with that system was that it now became the inmate's right to be enhanced, not the inmate's privilege to be earned. He didn't seem to have to do anything to show that he was willing to work hard, put the effort in to earn it and demonstrate that he was able to learn that positive behaviour has its rewards.

Even if the prison officer had the time, computer skills and the balls to place an inmate on the Basic regime (and then had the support of the governors – it's a time-consuming, difficult process), it's pointless. The inmate just had to say he couldn't cope, he wasn't breastfed as a child, his great-uncle twice removed died eighteen years before he was born, his guinea pig died when he was five, and the powers that be would take pity and allow him to have a television to help him 'cope'. Which then pisses off the inmates who have put the time and effort in to earn their television, making them wonder what the point is in bothering.

Hotel rooms

When I started working as a prison officer, the inside of a large Victorian prison didn't particularly take me by surprise. I had seen the inside of a prison on the television, in the 1969 film *The Italian Job* and Ronnie Barker's comedy series *Porridge*. Apparently, *Porridge* was once (and still is, I hear) used as a training aid for new recruits, and for me, walking onto the wing was like walking onto one of those film sets.

Wooden floors, wooden cell doors, wrought-iron railings and suicide netting. The cells were spartan: a bed, chair, table, small locker and a picture board. Personal items might include a cassette player and/or a battery-operated radio, a few books, some photos and toiletries. Oppressive and depressing, the prison seemed designed to be so bloody horrible and unpleasant that you wouldn't want to spend any longer there than you really had to.

Inmates now had power in their cells, kettles, flat-screen televisions, DVDs, games consoles, CD players, quilts. I've been in cells that have had the best quality Bose sound systems, Rolex watches and designer labels. There's even been talk of giving them phones in their cells. The emphasis now was to give the inmates everything they could possibly want so that they should want for nothing.

The thinking behind this seemed to be that if they had absolutely everything, they wouldn't have anything to complain about. They wouldn't want to escape, fight, steal, riot or rampage. They would be happy in their little cell, which should in turn mean they wouldn't have the urge to get up to no good. They would be content, happy and relaxed inmates, and pose far fewer problems for the far fewer prison officers to deal with.

Does it work? Does it hell. The old saying, 'Give him an inch and he'll take a yard,' might well have been coined with the prisoner in mind. Time and again I have come across prisoners on their umpteenth sentence. In fact, it is rare indeed to find an inmate on a wing who is in for the first time; they aren't in the slightest bit fazed about doing a bit of bird.

Officer or porter?

Head office seemed to see the inmates as cost–effective units, part of a convoluted business plan, while the longer-serving officers saw them for what they were, convicted criminals. But that didn't appear likely to last long, not only because of the instructions we'd been given to address an inmate as 'Mr', and to treat them as equals with respect and kindness; there was also the bizarre practice that I witnessed today, which has become a more common sight of late.

I saw an officer escorting an inmate from reception to the wing, struggling with the inmate's two prop bags★ like a hotel porter while unlocking the gates, while the inmate was just standing there watching with the single prop bag he'd deigned to carry. In the eyes of the inmates, we'd become more like a hotel's concierge than a prison officer, there to assist, help, problem-solve, arrange, care for and generally be at their beck and call. This was especially so if that officer was inexperienced in their eyes and naive in the ways of prison life. Once the inmate arrives from reception onto a wing, the first question is

---

★   A large sack-like polythene bag for carrying an inmate's property.

usually, 'Who is my personal officer? I've got some stuff that needs sorting.'

Lost or damaged property can be a big earner for the savvy inmate. The inmate simply breaks an item – his old, outdated radio or CD player – and then blames the officer who carried it. 'It must have been the officer, Guv. After all, it was working when we left reception.' The prison is then obliged to replace it with a new item. Stuff always goes missing during transfers or relocations and the inmate puts in a claim.

Accidents and injuries are other big money-spinners. Inmates would chuck tea, coffee – anything – on the floor and then feign injuries, saying they slipped and fell, screaming blue murder that there was no sign warning about the slippery surface. Or they might get 'injured' in the gym and hobble back, or accidentally on purpose trip or slip outside the office on some item or other – potholes or anything the enterprising inmate can utilise.

I heard the story that one year it was snowing and a meeting was held about whether or not to grit the paths. If they went ahead and gritted, and someone slipped on the gritted area, the prison would be liable; however, if they didn't grit and left snow and ice on the ground, and someone slipped (which they inevitably would), the prison wasn't liable. They gritted in the end, but it was a close-run thing.

Maintaining the barrier

Though the inmates have yet to get internet access (I'm sure it won't be long), they don't really need to if they pick the right officer to approach. The inmate steps into the wing office and says a cheery, 'Guv, while you're on the computer, you couldn't do us a favour and have a look to see if such and such is in stock?' Or, 'Guv, you couldn't find the phone number or address for me, could you?' I've seen officers spend forty plus minutes looking for stuff, inviting the inmates into the office while leaving confidential paperwork and reports in full view, or the other computer screen displaying confidential records (there were two computers in the office). With information about inmates on full display, you really need to be switched on and savvy, lest the curious inmate gets hold of stuff they shouldn't.

When I first arrived at Albany, I was working with another officer from the dispersal side of the prison and we counted the questions that we were asked in a two-hour window on a Sunday morning. On no fewer than seventy-two occasions did an inmate approach us in the office with some sort of opportunity to waste our time.

We'd both worked in the main prison, where we could spend an entire twelve-hour shift without a single inmate approaching us, and yet at Albany, with its more manipulative, creepy inmates, the standard practice from many staff seemed to be to encourage or accept it. The barrier between staff and inmates was flimsy to say the least, resulting in an apparent lack of respect, which was only ever going to cause trouble in the long run.

Reps

Wing reps were the bane of an officer's life. They seemed to have carte blanche to walk around the prison unescorted, clutching clipboards, wearing their own uniform (a coloured polo top). And when challenged, they'd mention a governor's or CM's name and we were obliged to back down. Gym reps, library reps, catering reps, measuring the quality of prisoners' lives (MQPL) reps, whose job it was to make sure the inmates were comfortable and wanted for nothing, and that the officers were actually doing their job to a reasonable standard, because if not, they would be reported to the wing CM. Yes, these inmates actually reported on the officers. Listeners, Shannon Trust (a charity supporting prisoners to learn to read), equalities rep, safer custody reps, veteran in custody support (VICS) reps. I counted fifteen religions, all of which had a rep. And, of course, not forgetting the Avon catalogue rep. It was just another area where any semblance of control had been eroded.

A terrible precedent

An inmate refused point-blank to bang up this afternoon because he wasn't happy about being told he was on the transfer list and would be moving to another prison. This one inmate managed to delay bang up by forty-five minutes, resulting in us all being late off duty. Even after being given a direct order, he refused, telling the officer to 'poke it'.

One of the CMs appeared and spoke to the inmate, assuring him that he would look into it. The inmate was seemingly rewarded for his behaviour by being taken off the transfer list. He would remain where he was, and the CM further assured him that there would be no nicking – he wouldn't be placed on report.

In the process, he'd set the other inmates a terrible precedent, which would make it very hard for any officer to nick an inmate for refusing to bang up. After all, they would rightly reason that what's good enough for one should be good enough for all. We were pissed off and late off duty, while he was left happy and content.

Segregation and Rehabilitation unit

One of the most mystifying management decisions during my time in the service was the decision to reduce the cell capacity in the Seg unit to just four cells some time ago. This would, apparently, show head office that the prison was run so well that the Seg unit was required only on extremely rare occasions, and only ever as a last resort. So well behaved were the inmates in this governor's prison, went the logic, that only four cells were required.*

The Seg unit, chokey or block was normally a place that any inmate wanted to avoid, an austere and unpleasant shithole that served as a deterrent and punishment. Back in the day, the officers who worked there enforced the rules with a rod of iron. They were the hard men and each officer in the Seg unit not only had to volunteer to work there, but also had to be accepted by the other Seg unit officers. As I've mentioned throughout, if they raised the alarm, it was inevitably for something serious. They took pride in keeping things in-house and running a tight ship.

However, along with the cell-space reduction, the decision was made to rename the Seg unit the less intimidating – and certainly more confusing – SARU, which stands for Segregation and Rehabilitation Unit. It didn't quite roll off the tongue in the same way. And this gentler 'rebrand'

---

* Every Seg unit was obligated to have one empty cell available at all times, just in case.

of the Seg didn't just stop with the name change; it called for a 'gentler', less intimidating regime and officers. The old-school, no-nonsense, hard-as-nails screws were replaced almost en masse to see in this softer regime with officers with, shall we say, a slightly more diplomatic and under-standing approach to the needs of the poor, misunderstood unfortunates in the 'care' of the SARU.

The reality, as ever, was somewhat different. Inmates who had assaulted other inmates, threatened staff, smashed things up, committed sexual assaults, brewed hooch or been guilty of bullying were now, owing to such a shortage of space in the SARU, having to be located on the wing. And it didn't take the inmates long to get up to speed on this and know they now had a licence to do likewise. The better-behaved inmates were now having to live on the same wing that their attacker lived; hooch-brewing inmates enjoyed goading their reporting officer, safe in the knowledge that it was extremely unlikely the officer could do anything about it and even if they did, they couldn't be located in the block because there were no empty cells.

Like so many other terrible decisions in the prison, it was eventually made clear what a complete fuck-up it was and the Seg unit was soon given more cell space. However, the softer regime meant it was never a deterrent, because they had virtually the same privileges as inmates on a normal wing. The only difference was that they were away from a crowded, noisy wing, which actually made it very appealing to some. Many Seg unit inmates were more than happy to have time out from the pressures of their regular wing and often treated the Seg unit as a bit of R & R.

More than once, an inmate who wanted a bit of 'time away' from the wing would say to an officer, 'Get me down the block.' Unfortunately, it had to be explained that he couldn't just go 'down the block', as we had to have a reason for taking him there. He had to be placed on report (even then it wasn't guaranteed), so the inmate would then – and rather annoyingly – do something to get nicked, tying us up with unnecessary paperwork for the next hour and a half.

An extremely confused, garbled transmission came over the radio today just as I made my way onto the wing to start my shift. The only bit we could make out was, 'Urgent assistance, education.' This was strange, if only because the education department at that time of day had no inmates. Were the staff fighting? Was there a fire or a medical emergency? The alarm bell went off, so another officer and I ran down the corridor, passing the one inmate who was waiting to get into his wing.

On arriving at education, the officer who was first on scene shouted, 'Who's the inmate in the corridor?' We didn't know who he was and neither of us had taken much notice of him, but at least we knew which wing he had gone on. It turned out that that inmate had apparently just beaten the shit out of a female teacher, a lovely middle-aged lady, who was only five foot three and with a heart of gold. An easy target for a spineless coward.

She had been beaten to the ground and was covered in claret. Her hands were in a bad way, as she had used them in a vain attempt to protect her face, and she had a deep, nasty-looking gash on her left eye. As more staff arrived, I went back to the only wing that the suspect could have entered. I asked the officer who it was and they told me it was an inmate by the name of LB.

This surprised me a little. This inmate was in the Seg unit as far as I was aware and had been for some considerable time, because he had previously assaulted and threatened staff, as well as spending some eight hours 'at height', threatening to jump. He could not or would not conform or follow the regime. He was an unpleasant, dangerous inmate who didn't hide the fact. He had made it quite clear that he would do anything and everything he could to disrupt the prison. Even in the block he was disruptive.

The managers in their infinite wisdom had apparently decided that to have a disruptive inmate in the Seg for as long as LB had been wasn't looking good for the oh-so important KPIs (key performance indicators). So as part of the 'appeasement policy', yet another 'special' deal was struck with LB. If he 'promised to behave and be a good boy', he could come out of the Seg unit (which had blatantly failed as any form of punishment, because he had been given the TV, showers and the rest; he was more than happy in there). Not only that, but he was also given his old cleaning job back, in the corridor. It was a trusted position and one from which he had been sacked on no less than three occasions because of his appalling behaviour.

He, of course, readily agreed to all of it. A number of the other inmates were royally and rightly pissed off and complained, if only because he was walking around and gloating about it. Likewise, the staff complained, not only because he was seen to be taking the piss, but because they also knew that it was just a matter of time before he crossed the line again. It was just a question of how badly and at whose cost.

This assault on the teacher happened a mere day and a half later. It was premeditated and ruthless. He engaged her in conversation and asked if she had a radio on her. When she replied that she hadn't, thus confirming that she wasn't able to summon help, the fists flew. It was her blood-curdling screams that had alerted staff.

The medics saw to her and she was taken to an outside hospital, while we could barely control our rage at the stupidity of the decision and how unnecessary it all was. A cowardly scumbag like LB should never in a million years have been in a position to do it in the first place. There would have been absolutely no chance of this happening earlier in the service.

The beating he inflicted was so bad that the teacher never returned to work. The case went to court, and he was given an extra twenty-three weeks on his sentence and fined £115. She, however, was left a broken woman with a career in tatters. Justice my arse!

Mistaken identity

One of the female OSGs was subjected to a torrent of verbal abuse during the night while doing her roll check. Threats were made and the cell door was kicked several times, all in an attempt to intimidate and scare. After completing the roll, she wrote out an Incentives and Earned Privilege (IEP) warning (a scheme whereby inmates earn certain privileges – back in the day, it would have been a nicking, but these were now all but worthless). Three of these warnings – for warnings read chances – would result in the inmate eventually being placed on the most Basic regime, and this was now his second.

He was nothing but a bully who hated females, loved himself and had an imposing presence. An arrogant Cockney gobshite who had done enough bird to realise, come the morning, that he might have just fucked up and it wouldn't be long before he was on Basic, but as usual, he wasn't the least bit worried about the consequences. It was simply a case of getting someone lower down the food chain to take the blame. True to form, today another inmate came to the office and explained that, would we believe it, it was him who had called the OSG all sorts of unpleasant names and threatened her, and it was him that had kicked the door. This inmate's cell was on the other side of the landing; his first language wasn't English and it certainly wasn't Cockney gobshite; he was close to tears and, coincidently, he had a nasty-looking lump under his left eye.

The CM of the wing was young and newly promoted way above his ability. To be fair, I think he realised it. He wasn't a people person, was never keen to look you in the eye and couldn't make a decision to save his life, but he was shit-hot on a computer, could quote the prison service rules and regulations verbatim, and had sycophancy down to an art form. In other words, a perfect prison service candidate for promotion.

He read through the IEP warning from the OSG, read the evidence and interviewed both of the inmates concerned (he never interviewed the OSG), and came to the only conclusion he could: the OSG was mistaken. She had got it all wrong. And the imposing, arrogant inmate with a history of bullying was the victim of her obvious mistake.

And back to the Seg unit

Following the assault on the teacher, the penny finally dropped. The ex-Seg unit staff – the old-school, no nonsense officers with a slightly more 'in your face' atti-tude – were asked to return to work there and get it back to how it was, with a tighter regime. It was an acknowledgement, at least, of how bad things had got. Let's see how long it lasts.

Sure enough, it turned out to be a short-lived acknowledgement: the managers couldn't keep their noses out and within six months, staff were thoroughly pissed off with their continual interference.

Being a good boy

'Balotelli' was an inmate who was a menace to everyone. He had a history of sexual assaults against women, though he didn't discriminate between genders: he was actually inside for raping a young male. During his time at Parkhurst he had touched, groped, pestered and assaulted just about every female he came into contact with. Around men he was a pain in the arse, but as soon as a female appeared, his whole demeanour changed, and he became polite, chatty, smiling and engaging. He genuinely seemed to believe he was God's gift.

Balotelli had been on the Basic regime for the allotted twenty-eight days, when O1 walked onto the wing this afternoon. This CM was a lovely fella, softly spoken, polite and kind to all, not unlike Mr Barrowclough in *Porridge*. Unfortunately, these traits, though extremely commendable outside the prison, were seen as nothing more than weaknesses ripe for exploitation.

Balotelli immediately collared him and explained that he had been on Basic for some time and was due for a review. The CM listened, took on board what he had said, checked PNOMIS and decided that if he was a good boy and promised to behave himself, he would 'give him a chance' and take him off Basic. He could have his television and go to the gym, but if he was naughty, the gym would be taken off of him. Balotelli thanked him and promised to be a very good boy indeed.

A leopard doesn't change its spots

True to his word, Balotelli behaved . . . long enough to have a single gym session. He'd gloated and laughed when he was taken off Basic, mainly because, not twenty-four hours previously, another CM had decided to leave him on Basic for another week because his behaviour was so bad (and hadn't, as yet, had time to update PNOMIS to that effect). But Balotelli had seen a chance. And with no regular wing staff on duty, he went for it. The other inmates were pissed off and the regular wing staff paid the price. He made a female officer's shift as unpleasant as possible for her: following her around, trying to get just a little too close for comfort. He also threw a bin full of food down the stairs and started making threats. He was back on Basic by the end of the day.

A month later

Balotelli had been emboldened of late and was overly confident, increasing his pestering, stalking behaviour with the wing's only female officer. We could see disaster looming and as concerned colleagues, we needed to do something about it. We reported each and every concern, highlighting every instance, and inundated the governors with paperwork. They were snowed under with the avalanche of paperwork we produced, warning after warning about his increasing threat to female staff. Eventually, and only after several meetings, a decision was made. Balotelli was to be moved and relocated to another wing today. He was informed that he would be moving and told to pack his kit, which he did without complaint.

When the time finally came to move him, he refused, barricaded himself in his cell and threatened all sorts of violence. A C & R team was assembled, the cell door was removed and in they went. However, it didn't go according to plan.

The first person in the cell was the 'shield man'. The textbook approach would be for him to inch his way forwards into the cell with a large, super-strong Perspex shield that would be placed against the inmate in a firm but forceful manner, thereby restricting the inmate's movement and ability to fight or struggle. The other two officers would then use approved techniques to restrain the inmate further before handcuffs were applied and the inmate was escorted out. In reality, however, the shield man was usually the biggest, strongest lump available. He would enter the cell at a great rate of knots and firmly push and hold the inmate against the wall before the two other officers would eventually apply wrist locks after a long and often desperate struggle. The cuffs would then finally be put on.

On this particular occasion, the shield man slipped on the cell floor that had been booby-trapped with baby lotion or something similar, and he went straight down. The barricade and debris made things difficult for the team but easy for Balotelli, who was in the mood for a fight. One officer, of slightly diminutive stature, grabbed him in a bear hug and hung on for dear life; the other officer was wrestling with furniture. Somehow, Balotelli got out of the cell.

He didn't get far, with two physical education instructors waiting outside the cell, one of whom was a C & R instructor, and thankfully, they managed to restrain him and take control of the situation. He was taken out to the back of the wing and straight into a waiting van, and then into the Seg unit. Or so we all thought.

Instead, it was decided to locate him on a normal wing. The Seg unit was for naughty people and Balotelli didn't seem to meet the criteria. Refusing to move, barricading himself in his cell, fighting staff, being sexually and overtly predatory to females still didn't warrant him being located in the Seg unit. He just wasn't naughty enough, apparently.

The wing he was placed on just forty minutes after his tussle with staff had at least three female officers on it. He was in his element. We were all in a state of shock. His appalling behaviour had been condoned rather than punished and this master manipulator had once again manipulated his way out of trouble.

Breaking down barriers

Today, one young female officer thought she was doing the right thing when she went into an inmate's cell to talk to him and try to 'gain his trust and break down barriers'. Unfortunately, this inmate was a rapist with multiple convictions, who realised that some of the young staff were a little naive and consequently ripe for exploitation and manipulation, to put it mildly. He managed to coax this young officer into his cell, where he spun his tale of woe. She sat on his bed and comforted him by giving him a cuddle, and she came out of the cell pleased with herself for a job well done. He, however, came out with a hard-on.

Truly screwed

Trafficking offered some very severe consequences, and for female officers they could be even worse. If they got sucked in or blackmailed into trafficking, the price for keeping quiet could be anything from even more trafficking to a grope or worse. Some inmates were master manipulators with nothing to lose and a lot to gain; they had the uncanny ability to smell fear and spot a victim a mile away.

A female cooking instructor was sentenced to two months in prison for smuggling a mobile phone in for an inmate. A lovely but vulnerable woman, she suffered from low confidence and self-worth, while the inmate was a sex offender and, as is often the case, one of these parasites can spot a potential victim a mile away.

With a degree of flattery and above-and-beyond help-fulness, he wormed his way in and gained her trust. She enjoyed the attention and when she informed the inmate that she would be on leave for a couple of weeks, his master plan came to fruition. He told her that he was going to miss her and would be suitably sad in her absence; if only they could keep in touch, he continued, no one would ever need to know. 'It would be our own special little secret,' he said. She agreed and smuggled a phone in.

She went on holiday and seemed to have spent most of it on the phone to him, because it was revealed that some six or seven hundred messages were exchanged between them. The inmate now had her hook, line and sinker. He suggested that she give him her credit card details so he could purchase some apps for the phone and the penny finally dropped for the instructor. She said no, so he threatened her with telling the prison that she had smuggled the phone in and that they had had sex – he would show them the texts and her knickers (yes, he had in his possession a couple of pairs of her knickers). She was well and truly screwed (no pun intended), but she finally had the good sense to see it and go to the police.

Water off a duck's back

The NHS-run HCC staff saw the inmates as being patients, rather than inmates who require treatment. Not only did they address them as such – Mr or their first name – but, rightly or wrongly, they also treated them as such. The education department saw them as students. The governors seemed to see them as poor unfortunates who needed understanding, help and rehabilitation.

A female governor was today doing her rounds, when one inmate started shouting obscenities at her. She never batted an eyelid and so the language – and the invitations to all manner of grotesque and deviant sexual acts she had coming her way, according to the inmate – got even more foul and depraved. She never challenged the inmate, warned him or nicked him, and while she may have had her reasons for this, I fear that through her inaction the inmate may have got the impression she condoned that kind of behaviour. Did the inmate now think it fair game to verbally abuse any and all of the female staff? What about the inmates who were no doubt listening? As officers we were told, encouraged and instructed to challenge disruptive behaviour.

A scrap on the exercise yard

After arriving at work after an enjoyable week off, I was catching up on the gossip and rumours doing the rounds.

Screws love nothing more than a bit of gossip, as it's enough to get us through most shifts, and we never let something as mundane as the truth get in the way of a good rumour in a prison. Apparently, a workshop instructor had been suspended for sunbathing behind his workshop in the nude. Then I was told about an incident on the exercise yard the day before.

While exercise was in progress, the supervising staff were busy moaning about anything and everything (I forgot to mention that we like moaning as much as we like gossiping), when a fight suddenly broke out. The alarm was raised, and the staff dived in and attempted to break it up. One of the fighters stopped and tried to back off, but the other one was having none of it. Three staff grabbed him and still he wouldn't stop. Thankfully, he wasn't tooled up, but fists and feet were swinging.

The staff eventually wrestled him to the ground, but he continued to struggle and only after he had finally tired himself out did he give up the ghost. The SO, however, was still in full-blown wrestling mode, desperately trying to gain control of his leg. He was now, however, several feet away from the inmate, but to his credit, and only thanks to his tenacious spirit, he finally managed to gain control of the inmate's prosthetic leg.

The day an inmate won the lottery

Collins was an inmate from Liverpool. The archetypal Scouser, full of wit and wisdom, he was also a royal pain in the arse. He was constantly up to no good and always happy to make life difficult for staff. He had done enough bird to know how the system worked, how to exploit it and how to piss off the officers without ever quite crossing the line. He was a big lump of an inmate and used his physical presence to great effect, bullying and poncing (borrowing or acquiring) his way through each and every one of his many sentences. He was always poncing off someone and he would invariably run up debts, go down the block and get moved on or transferred out.

The staff on D wing were fed up with him, but Collins never actually did enough for the staff to do anything about it. However, one officer who was equal in Collins's resourcefulness decided it was payback time, so he 'accidently' dropped a fake scratch card outside of Collins's cell while he was unlocking the landing. Collins was as sneaky as he was predictable, and he played his part well. The moment he stepped out of his cell, he stood on the scratch card while the officer had his back to him.

Once the officer had finished unlocking, Collins returned to his cell with his scratch card and, would you believe it, promptly won the £50,000 jackpot. Now, the staff could enjoy seeing Collins's squirming and desperate scheming to get the £50,000 winning ticket out of the prison and cashed, but not before getting himself into even more debt with the promise of repaying all previous and future debts with his win.

He was soon transferred out and we heard that at his next prison he was bragging about how much of a windfall he was about to receive, which raised concerns to the point that staff started monitoring his phone calls. One of which was to his kids, telling them that when he got out (which was in five months' time) he would be taking them to Disney World, Florida. So we now had it confirmed that he had got the card out of our prison and it was still in his possession. Many of the staff on D wing would have given anything to be a fly on the wall when he found out he'd been had.

CHAPTER 12

Sentence Served

Not fit for purpose

The percentage of prison officers who join the service but don't want to or simply can't actually work on a wing full of prisoners is frightening. I was told by one governor that out of the 220 uniformed staff at HMP Parkhurst and its sister site, Albany, there were sixty-seven officers who, for whatever reason, couldn't work in certain areas of the prison. The reasons ranged from threats made by inmates, members of staff not getting on (usually some screw screwing another screw's wife) and injury, to investigations, stress or breakdowns.

On top of that, we had some twenty-eight officers promoted on a temporary basis. These were usually fairly new officers, often with less than a couple of years in. The newish officers were on a lot less money, with a smaller pension and no lump sum final pay-off, and were often over-promoted to the rank of CM or above. One new officer with just *twenty-four weeks* in the job applied for promotion to the rank of CM just to make up for their differing pay scale.*

---

* When I started you had to get out of your year's probationary period then be an officer for at least seven years before you could even think of promotion; you need the experience of working on the landings and the respect of your colleagues.

Some officers were in positions way above their ability, hopelessly out of their depth thanks to a promotion technique that required them to be nothing more than a sort of sycophantic suppository, seemingly prepared to sell their soul and agree wholeheartedly to whatever bullshit came their way. More times than I care to think about, a young officer seeking promotion didn't need ability, but they did need to be malleable, amenable and prepared to toe the party line, otherwise they simply wouldn't be promoted. The trouble with in-house promotion was that a weak, ineffectual and bullying governor would always promote the yes-men to make his or her life a lot easier. After all, they were easy to blame and amenable to bad practices such as unlocking a wing without enough staff, and they could be pushed around and used as scapegoats, knowing they had little or no choice and even less experience.

The old days of promotion on ability or merit seemed to be another thing consigned to the long-forgotten past. The prison service seemingly relied on the 'Peter Principle' for promotion, a management concept developed by the Canadian academic Laurence J. Peter, which states that 'in a hierarchy every employee tends to rise to his level of incompetence'. Nowhere did that feel truer than in the modern prison service. The good SO or CM needed the ability to say yes or no, be firm and decisive; strength of character and a firm hand were required to stand up to something that was blatantly wrong. These were the exact characteristics that a weak, ineffectual governor didn't want.

These promotions, combined with the inability of staff to work in certain areas, meant that we might have had a total staffing level of 220 uniforms on paper, but in reality, we had a shortfall of ninety-five. I'm sure head office were only aware of the fact that on paper there were more than enough officers.

It's easy to look at the past through rose-tinted glasses, particularly for an old 'dinosaur' screw like me with more than twenty-five years in the job. But when I joined the service, HMP Parkhurst had some 350 officers, the number one governor knew your name and for a job well done, he would come and speak to you to say thank you. Staffing levels had halved, prisoner numbers doubled and the number one was unlikely to know your name. The latest number one governor probably wouldn't know me from Adam. For a job well done you *might* get shopping vouchers, but I would sooner have a personal thank you from a governor that I respected. I hate shopping, as governors of the past would have known.

Bleedin' paperwork

I've lost count of the amount of times one of my colleagues or I have cut someone down who was attempting to hang themselves (regardless of whether it was a serious or half-hearted attempt), talked someone out of harming themselves or others, dealt with inmates refusing to bang up, had some 'unauthorised item' like a weapon or drugs handed in, stood in between tooled-up, fighting inmates, or defused all manner of potentially volatile situations without spending hours on paperwork afterwards. Years ago, I could put the kettle on and fill out a nicking sheet (to place an inmate on report) before the kettle had boiled. Today, the last nicking I gave out took forty-seven minutes to complete. And that was only after leaving the landing and eventually finding a computer.

Just think about that. If I give out three nickings this week (and God forbid any should happen ten minutes before the end of a shift), I will need to be away from the landing and on a computer for two and a half hours. And that's just one officer. Imagine half a dozen officers doing the same . . .

It used to be that you'd deliver the nicking sheet to the Seg unit, where the officers would then check it and make sure it was correct. But now, a nicking is so complicated and time-consuming, and thrown out for the most pedantic reasons – a capital letter wasn't used, an apostrophe was in the wrong place – and it's all just another exasperating example of the odds stacked against the officer and in favour of the inmate. In a seriously understaffed prison, paperwork is a bane and paperwork is a pain, and often just a waste of an officer's already limited time. Time that would be better spent on the landing watching, supervising, preventing, helping and deterring.

So you have to find other solutions to the problems inmates pose. If an inmate refuses to bang up, which is standard practice from an inmate testing the water, you don't bother arguing with him or try to convince him to go behind his door. It's simply not worth the effort. After all, the inmate has now put himself in a position where he can't be seen to back down in front of the other inmates; he's prepared for an argument and is ready for the inevitable confrontation. But I usually just take the wind out of his sails by telling him to grab a chair and make himself comfortable. I don't argue, don't react. I know he'll get bored. Then, once the rest of the wing is banged up and his audience has gone, he usually just goes away, feeling stupid and slightly annoyed that it didn't have the desired effect, but not before putting on a good, loud vocal display, making sure his peers know that he was last away and had showed the screws. And even if he doesn't go away and decides to fight or argue, you now have the staff to move him.

When it's time to unlock the inmates, of course, then you have your turn. You unlock the trouble-making inmate last and thus claim back the several minutes he owes you. Those minutes of lost association, the fact that he's now last in the queue for the phones, the gym, the pool room and the showers usually cures him of wanting to be the last away come bang-up time. Problem solved and no paperwork involved.

Lights, camera, action!

Another day, another innovation in the prison service. Body Worn Video Cameras (BWVC) had the potential to be a great aid to the understaffed prison, though certainly not as great an aid as more staff would be. By wearing these cameras, we would potentially have video and audio evidence of an inmate's poor and threatening behaviour, or justification for some of the actions we had to take on the job. Likewise, they could be an invaluable deterrent, with an inmate less likely to put himself in a situation where he couldn't dispute or deny his actions. They were, in theory, a great idea.

But, like so many of the prison service's well-intentioned ideas, the practicalities made their use almost farcical. The training was the first stumbling block. The new officers at the training college apparently received a whole morning's worth of tuition on the use of the BWVC, the policy, legislation, Data Protection Act, Freedom of Information Act and a whole load more various Acts, including everyone's favourite: the 1998 Human Rights Act. The vast majority of the officers already in post at the prison received what appeared to be a bastardised version of the training. And those officers who had somehow managed to avoid the obligatory tuition got a crash course that consisted of: 'To switch on, press this button; to switch off, press that button.'

At the end of training, we were asked the obligatory, 'Has anyone got any questions?' This was never a good thing to say to a bunch of cynical old screws, especially when the question was coming from a newly promoted, out-of-his-depth CM. Half a dozen hands went up.

'If we film someone else lying to an inmate or a member of staff, could I have access to the footage?'

'What if the camera accidentally films something like us using the toilet?'

To this latter question, we were offered half-hearted assurances that any accidental, potentially embarrassing footage would be seen by no one except authorised personnel. There was a definitive collective sigh of, 'Yeah, right!'

You've been framed

The cameras were to be switched on and used for any incident with an inmate. The cameras were, we were told, robust. They were also large, cumbersome, heavy blocks of plastic that had a tendency to switch themselves on if knocked, rattled or bashed. Unfortunately, our white shirts weren't designed for these cumbersome objects and clipping them on to the shirts wasn't the best of ideas, especially when moving fast or engaged in something physical. They easily became detached or were accidentally switched on.

Their fallibility had been highlighted many times over the first couple of weeks of their use. The first time was when an inmate was inadvertently filmed during a strip-search. On another occasion, it had switched itself on while an officer not known for his high fitness levels was running – sorry, making his way as quickly and as safely as possible★ – to an alarm bell. While gates were being unlocked, the camera picked up the vital footage of the heavy breathing, wheezing and coughing of the unfit officer. In fact, running to alarm bells seemed to set the cameras off regularly. And to cap it all, there was the occasion when a young female officer filmed herself getting undressed in the gym changing room for a lunchtime run. With no delete button, the only way the footage could be cleared was by one of those special and mysterious authorised personnel we'd heard about earlier.

Another thing the inmates soon realised was how they could use them to their advantage. They could punch an officer without a camera or before it was turned on, then raise their hands. No retaliatory action could be taken, after all, as all the viewer would see was an inmate with raised hands. Inmates would shout, 'Stop, stop, officer! You are hurting me.' Or, 'Why did you punch me just now?' Or even accuse officers of using racist language, all for the benefit of the cameras.

All of these incidents occurred within weeks of the introduction of the cameras, leaving officers having to

---

★ Officially, we weren't supposed to run.

prove the incidents the inmates referred to *didn't* actually happen. It felt like more staff were now suspended and under investigation than ever before. It was virtually impossible to prove you *didn't* actually say something.

Drug testing

One of the officers working in the mandatory drug-testing unit informed us today that, out of the twenty-six positive drug tests carried out in a single month, only four had actually been found guilty. A staggering twenty-two positive tests were thrown out or dismissed owing to the paperwork and/or evidence not being submitted on time (often, this was down to staff shortages), or the reams of complicated paperwork not being completed properly.

The Home Office number crunchers were blissfully unaware – or at least we hoped they were unaware – of the fact that so many guilty inmates were getting away with taking drugs. As far as the number crunchers were concerned, only four inmates were guilty of taking an illicit drug. The prison service obviously now looked good and could, with a clear conscience, inform the world that there really wasn't that much of a problem with drugs in this particular prison. Meanwhile, it was business as usual for the pushers and abusers.

Reoffending

When I first started working as a prison officer I was shocked by the amount of inmates who had reoffended. In my naivety, I had thought that prison and incarceration would be so unpleasant that no one in their right mind would ever want to return. Once should have been enough – or so I thought.

When I looked at the statistics, the proven reoffender rate for adults released from custodial sentence between January and February 2017 who reoffend within twelve months was *47.9 per cent.** Now, I'm aware of the much-quoted line popularised by Mark Twain, 'There are three kinds of lies: lies, damned lies and statistics', but in my personal experience I felt that well over half of the prison population were repeat offenders. They might not be overjoyed or happy about doing yet another sentence, but they weren't exactly worried, either. At worst, it's an annoyance and, bizarrely, at best, it's a great business opportunity.

That might appear to be a really silly thing to say, but one particular prisoner was actually heard bragging about how happy he was to return to prison because he can easily make £80,000 a year. He even had the cheek to ask if he could have his old cell back. And he wasn't the only one. For some, it was a great way of making money. Think about it: in prison he has a ready-made market, a willing workforce happy to smuggle, hide and distribute any illegal items, which could be anything from mobile phones to porn, drugs, tobacco, weapons, hooch or anything you can think of. Everything and anything was available for a price. I was told that half an ounce of tobacco would fetch £50 a couple of weeks prior to the smoking ban

---

* Proven Reoffending Statistics Quarterly Bulletin, January 2017 to March 2017. Ministry of Justice. January 2019 https://assets. publishing.service.gov.uk/government/uploads/system/uploads/ attachment_data/file/775079/proven_reoffending_bulletin_January_ to_March_17.pdf

being introduced, when everyone was panic buying, so the markup and profit margin on illicit items made the whole enterprise worth the effort.

Who left the gate unlocked?

A 'stand still roll check' happens when every prisoner in the prison has to be banged up and/or accounted for. Occasionally, it happens when the numbers don't tally: the workshops or gym might inform the control room that they have X amount of inmates, while each of the respective wings have informed the control room that they have sent X amount to work, and the numbers don't add up. However, these days, the vast majority of the time a 'stand still roll check' was done because some idiot had left a gate unlocked – a major breach, as anyone could just walk through the open gate.

As soon as it happens, we have to bring everything to a standstill to count every single inmate and report the numbers to the control room. This happened again today and it seemed to be happening two or three times a month at the moment. I didn't know if it was the training (or lack of it), the quality of the staff or a combination of the two.

Government clamp-down

One of the national newspapers today proudly proclaimed that the recently appointed prisons minister Rory Stewart would be clamping down: 'Prisoners will be forced to clean up rubbish-strewn jail yards as part of a "back to basics" crackdown.' Hurrah! I hear the readers cry. This guy means business.

It's just so unfortunate that this particular 'something' has been done for years. This was simply a yards party, a job that I, along with every other NEPO, was given when I first joined the service in 1992. Some twenty-six and a half years previously. So, for us, this was just confirmation that the so-called powers that be didn't have a clue about what actually happens inside a prison and yet they were tasked with coming up with ideas to make the system work, a system that they'd spent years breaking themselves.

Through the keyhole

The amount of staff who now walked around with their keys on display was frightening. It was drummed into us from the beginning of my time in the service that keys must be kept out of view from inmates, for obvious reasons. Some inmates can read keys and copy them, which was what was rumoured to have happened during the escape in 1995. It only took a short while for the inmate to be able to copy the keys. Like radios, keys should be attached to the person at all times. But now civvies, uniformed staff and even some governors seem to think it's fine to have them in the shop window for the inmates to have a good look at. One new officer was caught the other day actually throwing his unclipped keys up into the air on his way to the gate, happy to be at the end of his shift.

I've had a NEPO due to start at training school next week shadowing me today. He has been shadowing and observing life on the landings for a few weeks, but today he asked me which key he needed to use to get into an office. I said, 'Use the A suite.' He looked even more confused before asking which one that was. He had been issued with a complete set of keys, including a cell key, without knowing what they were for.

When I started, I was chucked in at the deep end and either got it right or wrong; it was a case of sink or swim. My colleagues wanted to see how I managed, how I reacted, and the fact that I had to work it out and think for myself worked. It was a tried-and-tested, though somewhat unofficial, training method. A method that worked. Try that approach now, however, and it felt like you'd be up for bullying, and the NEPO's cock-up would be considered your fault. They have to be guided gently, looked after, cared for and, frankly, mollycoddled.

Prison-issue camouflage

Inmates by their very nature are always up to no good. They will, as a matter of course, take any opportunity to conceal, disguise or mislead. They are nothing if not ingenious in their ability to hide just about anything, including themselves. The last thing any officer would want to do is make an inmate's penchant for hiding things any easier.

Unfortunately for us, one of the governors didn't appear to have thought this through. He had signed off a request for one of our workshops to start producing camouflage netting. The kind of stuff the military use. Just plain old netting in itself would be a fantastic climbing aid to throw over razor wire, but this was camouflage netting, whose sole purpose was to hide or disguise the presence of something that you wouldn't wish to be found. We already spent an inordinate amount of time and energy searching for and looking for things that inmates tried to hide, and yet the senior decided to allow inmates to produce an item designed to help and encourage them in their nefarious ways.

May the force be with you

Today, there was a big hoo-ha because two young officers barely out of their teens went into town during their lunch break, and while in uniform – which is always inadvisable for obvious reasons. The fact that an officer would need telling that is frightening.★ Anyway, they decided to have a pretend sword fight in the local supermarket car park using their extendable batons,† much like a child would play with their toy *Star Wars* light sabre.

Map reading

A young officer had been in the job for a little over three months, but even after all that time she still couldn't tell you where the workshops were. When she was told again today, she said she wouldn't be able to remember it and would have to draw a map of the prison to carry around with her. You don't have maps of a high-security prison on your person! This was frightening but not unusual. When I started the PO would ask me where various places in the

---

★ I NEVER wore mine outside of the prison in all my years of service; but then I never told anyone I worked in the prison service – I was a civil servant as far as anyone else was concerned, and even my next-door neighbours didn't know until I was in the paper for winning a 352-mile footrace in the Arctic.
† These batons were introduced in the late-1990s and replaced the wooden staves, effectively a short baton (and incidentally far more practical for the job).

prison were, or how we got from one location to another, to make sure I knew where I was going.

Another worrying thing it displayed was that should an alarm bell go off, she wouldn't have known which way to go. It was hammered into us that the first thing you do when you arrive on an unfamiliar wing is remember the exit points (escape routes), fire points and alarm bells. You should know these within minutes of arriving onto a wing.

2019

Resilience

A NEPO recently made a formal complaint against an officer because he laughed when he didn't know how to use the photocopier and I learnt today that the officer has now been placed under investigation for 'bullying'. Practical competence, like mental robustness, no longer seemed to be deemed to be valuable assets. The days of the screw with balls the size of coconuts and a hard, no-nonsense edge felt like they were long gone.

In recent times I've seen officers crying because an inmate's budgie had died, because an inmate had shouted at them and for any number of reasons while on duty. It became the norm and it seemed that many of the new officers lacked the mental tenacity to cope with the harsher of realities of prison life. This isn't to belittle the staff who suffer genuine trauma, or those who suffer mental strain after years on the wing – the job does take its toll, especially in an understaffed, dangerous prison, and even the hardest officer can feel the burden. No, I'm talking about staff cracking under the first sign of anything disagreeable.

What did they think the job would entail? And why or how were they not told?

Some of the youngsters seemed to come into the job in the mistaken belief that the black-and-white uniform was like a Marvel superhero's costume, conferring instant respect upon the wearer, a shield protecting them from harm. This ridiculous confidence was often coupled with too much time spent playing computer games, and not enough time spent developing things like patience, tact and diplomacy – basic interpersonal skills. Common sense and quick thinking in some of the officers seemed to be an alien concept.

The harsh reality of working in a prison is shocking for anyone, but for a millennial who still lives with their parents and whose main form of communication is through a smartphone, it must be doubly so. I realise how old and cynical this makes me sound, but the fact is that many of these staff get regraded to either the admin side of things or the OSG, which keeps them off the landings.

One of the new officers, who had arrived from Newbold Revel back in September 2018, told us that they were informed that out of every ten trainees, eight leave the service within the first year. An 80 per cent dropout rate seemed like a bloody expensive way of training two prison officers.

In 2018, we seemed to have a huge recruitment drive. I know I'm old, but looking at the millennial prison officer didn't exactly fill me or many of my colleagues with confidence. It seemed to me that this hurried approach to recruiting was very much a case of quantity over quality: get as many in to replace the undoubted shortfall and quickly get those boxes ticked. It was so unfair on both the new recruits and on us.

The desperation to get officers in post was such that the recruitment policy was farcical. The new recruits have to be computer savvy, of course. The initial application is now done online, which is only to be expected, and a big part of our job involves having to use computers for all the paperwork. But computers aren't the only part of the job. The role of a prison officer relies on interpersonal skills, the ability to interact and communicate with all manner of individuals: from the academically bright to the violent and dangerous thug. Not to mention the mentally ill, the illiterate, the non-English speakers and the career criminal. All kinds of personality type will at some time or other be encountered.

The initial job interview for the role of prison officer has been dispensed with, no doubt to save money and streamline the whole process, but I personally believe that the initial interview was one of the most important aspects of recruit-ment. My interview was more akin to an interrogation; trick questions, verbal aggression and no-win scenarios were all thrown at me, simply to see how I handled it. Would I buckle, cry, argue or lose my rag? They rightly needed to see the whites of my eyes and know that I wouldn't be intimidated, that I would be able to hold my own and remain calm during a verbal onslaught. The new officer, however, wouldn't actually be seen until after he or she got accepted for training for the job and turned up at the prison.

The process ends up being extremely unfair on the new recruit, who hasn't been tested properly to make sure he or she can deal with the real-life demands of the job, leaving many of them hopelessly out of their depth at the first sign of trouble. And it leaves us, in an already understaffed prison, with many (but by no means all) colleagues we can't rely on when things turn nasty, and not necessarily through any fault of their own. The process should be producing officers well suited to the harsh, bloody, confrontational realities they'll face inside a prison. Head office will proudly proclaim that the 2500 new prison officers are in post and they have met their promised target; they won't mention the numbers who have left the service, which by all accounts are far more than actually joined.

The strange thing was that to become an OSG, a role that doesn't actually involve working directly with inmates, the interview was, apparently, similar to the one we longer-serving officers endured: tough, tricky and more akin to an interrogation. Tough and tricky apparently wasn't something that the recent selection process should be for prison officers, lest any of them be unable to reach the necessary seemingly low standards required to make up the numbers.

I was due to leave the service later this year. My official retirement date was scheduled to be 27 September 2019, but it looked likely I could leave in July thanks to the hours I'd accrued. The 'appeasement policy' towards the inmates, the training of new staff, the weak and ineffectual management, the expectation on us to call inmates Mr, spending hours in an office on a computer, watching new staff knocking on cell doors and not dealing with confrontation . . . the list could go on. But the simple fact was that I wasn't enjoying the job any longer, and I hadn't for some time.

Send for the specialists!

The prison had its own DST, the elite specialists whose sole purpose was to search. They had done the courses and quite literally got the T-shirt: they had their own special uniform, dressing from head to toe in black. They even had bigger belts to carry the specialist bits of kit needed for such a prestigious and important role.

The trouble was that they were often officers who wouldn't or couldn't work on a wing, or who at least felt that working on an actual wing was for lesser mortals. I'd already had dealings with the DST when we were tackling the spice epidemic on the wing.

Today, we were given further insight into their highly trained specialist abilities. They arrived on the wing with their folders and reams of very important-looking paperwork. Their array of search kit was impressive. They were here, we were informed, to tick a box in the form of a tool check, which would then confirm that all the wing tools were accounted for. They set about their task with great gusto: scissors, nail clippers, darts, extension leads and gardening tools would all need to be seen and checked. After some considerable time, they had just about finished, satisfied that everything was as it should be except for the wing's lawn mower, a bright orange Flymo used for keeping the small garden beside the wing neat and tidy.

They couldn't find it and were quick to inform us that if the lawn mower was unaccounted for, there would be hell to pay. 'Who was the last inmate to use it?' they asked – always a helpful question when you're looking for something – and so they went on. An officer then asked, 'Have you checked the garden tool cabinet?' This was the 6-foot-high metal cage in which the DST had instructed us to store the lawn mower. Sure enough, sitting forlornly inside was the bright orange Flymo. We laughed. They didn't see the funny side.

Course work

Among our ranks we had a group of people who we referred to as the professional course attenders. These were the officers who attended any course going, from wheelchair pushing to drone watching, and from first aid to hostage negotiator, as well as the 'how to talk to an inmate nicely' course. A lot of courses on offer were irrelevant and taught by people who either personified the proverb 'those who can, do; those who can't, teach' or, if we're being polite, who didn't exactly have their heart in working on a wing full of inmates.

Even the obligatory annual C & R refresher was now so watered down that it actually bore no resemblance to what actually happened in a real-life 'take out' situation. C & R refreshers used to be realistic, hard and physical, acting out various violent and extremely realistic scenarios from 8 a.m. till late afternoon. Now, the morning was spent in the classroom, going through reams of paperwork and the dos and don'ts.

Many courses were totally irrelevant to our role as a prison officer, but attending them got the professional course attender away from the wing and the actual prisoners. It was becoming a rare thing indeed to actually find a prison officer who was happy to come in and simply do their shift on the wing.

Stop and search

I cycled into work this morning, had my shower in the block outside the prison as usual and, as happens every so often, was subjected to a staff search. One of the new officers beckoned me over, saying he had to search my small rucksack. He went through my soggy cycling gear, including my wet socks and a pair of underpants that, to my embarrassment, had seen better days. He worked on my wing, so we had a chat as he went through my stuff. I asked him if he knew what he was looking for and he admitted that he didn't. He had just been told to search us, but for what, he didn't have a clue.

When he returned to the wing later, I said to him, 'Didn't anybody explain to you what to look for?'

'No,' he said. 'I was just told that I'd be searching the staff.'

I then asked him, 'Have you ever brought anything into the prison that you shouldn't have?'

'No – never,' came his immediate answer.

As we were sitting next to the lockers and his was open, I pointed out that he had a glass container, which was a no-no. His defence was that it was only aftershave, which was another no-no, as it contained alcohol. There was a packet of chewing gum and a metal teaspoon in his locker, too, all prohibited items, and yet here he was doing the searching.

Equal ops

The prison service, like many companies today, has an obligation to be an equal opportunities employer, which is a commendable and fair approach to recruitment. However, it seems to me that like most things involving the prison service, it's done for the right reasons but with the wrong approach.

Shortly before I arrived at Albany, an OSG who had unfortunately lost an arm had been employed. He was a lovely fellow, friendly, efficient, keen as mustard and bloody hard-working. He was pleased as punch with being given the opportunity to work again. Unfortunately for him, one of the main parts of his job was escorting vehicles around the prison. This required two OSGs, one at the front of the vehicle and one at the back, with the one at the front opening the gates, and the one at the back closing and securing them. Only when the gate was secure would the OSG give the nod for the vehicle to move off.

These gates were huge metal things some 15 feet high and 8 feet across, and they weighed a ton. This was bad enough on a good day, but when it was a little breezy, they became nothing more than giant sails. The wind would catch them and it would become a slow-motion wrestling match. On top of that, it was a fiddly operation even if the weather was fine, inserting and turning a key, lifting and sliding a bolt across, often requiring a little jiggle, push and shove to line the locks up before the bolt could be slid across successfully.

It was bad enough for a two-armed man, but the one-armed man struggled and often couldn't manage. So the prison service, realising there was a problem and yet ever keen to be seen to be an equal opportunity employer, hired another OSG to assist the one-armed OSG, so that they now had three arms to do a two-armed job.

Driving test

Driving is an important part of an OSG's job. At Albany, a lot of the inmates were elderly, sick or hypochondriacs, and colostomy bags and catheters were *de rigueur*. All of which made for a lot of trips to the outside hospital, escorted by officers in a van driven by an OSG. The OSGs would also drive to the kitchen, which was about a quarter of a mile from the prison, and pick up the cooked meals for the prison.

One of the newer OSGs arrived for work today and was looking at the detail to see what job he would be doing the next day, when he noticed that he was down as the 'kitchen driver'. Slightly confused, he asked what this entailed and was told that it was a cushy number. 'You just drive the wagon to and from the kitchen, collecting and delivering the meal trollies for each of the wings.'

He then asked, 'When will I be taught how to drive?'

He had passed the necessary interviews and tests, but no one at any point had thought to ask him if he could drive. It was like employing a person to be a lifeguard but not checking that they could actually swim.

High and dry

We had another incident at height today, which have been happening regularly of late. Some idiot would climb up onto something, usually a roof – though what is deemed to be an incident at height is often something as mundane as a flight of stairs or the suicide netting – and then the inmate would make threats or demands, or even just vent their anger or frustration to get a point across to their captive audience. The serious ones were usually the pissed-off loners, who invariably tie a noose around their neck and pick a precarious position from which to get their point across.

Today, however, one of these idiots had got up onto a small roof by hoisting and pulling himself up (it was so low that it wasn't even a climb), whereupon he threatened to jump. He stayed up there until he ran out of things to say, and with the evening drawing in and teatime fast approaching, he decided to come down. One of the recently arrived NEPOs, with a little over three weeks in the job was so distraught by the day's horrendous events that he had to go home. He couldn't cope with such a 'cataclysmic incident'.

Indeed, this traumatised NEPO spent some time off on the sick before finally leaving the prison service, blaming the service for not caring enough about his well-being.

Never too late to learn

I had spent twenty-eight years working on one prison landing or another at both Parkhurst and Albany, nearly 8000 shifts during which I would deal with inmates of every type, colour, creed, sexual orientation, religious persuasion and personality type. Today, I was informed by the training department that I was to spend two days sitting in a classroom being taught how to talk to inmates by people who didn't work with inmates, just twenty weeks before I was due to retire. Now, I was finally going to see how it was really done.

Squeamish?

An inmate had to be taken to the outside hospital today for a routine colonoscopy, in which a camera was inserted into his bowels via the anal passage. One officer was fascinated and was watching the whole thing on the monitor, when the NEPO, who was actually handcuffed to the inmate, fainted and collapsed, nearly dragging both the inmate and the camera onto the floor.

Thankfully, the nurses intervened and helped the officer, averting a potentially dangerous situation. What the hell was this officer going to be like when there was a fight, a suicide, or some blood and guts to deal with on the job? It didn't bode particularly well if he couldn't even make it through a routine hospital procedure.

Shock horror!

Another display of how out of touch the national press were with what really happened in Britain's jails was today's 'shock horror!' story of dead rats being used to smuggle in drugs. The rats were caught, killed, gutted, stuffed and packed with drugs, then crudely stitched up and thrown over the prison perimeter wall to be collected and the contents sold on. A disgusting act according to both the press and readers, but for life inside it was normal practice and certainly nothing new – much like smuggling drugs into visits inside babies' nappies. Things like regurgitating and plugging might seem disgusting but, again, they were the norm inside.

Vaping

I was now three months away from retirement. The system was broken and I couldn't wait to get out, to be honest. I did a shift on my old wing in Parkhurst today. I stood on the landing reading the noticeboard, which proudly proclaimed, 'Vaping is only to be done in your cell and not on the landing.'

Thanks to the smoking ban, vaping has become incredibly popular in prison – just as it has outside in the real world – as part of the prison service's efforts to ease the inmates' transition from cigarettes. Even head office could see the dangers inherent in making prisons full of nicotine-addicted cons go cold turkey, so inmates were allowed to vape in their cells.

Standing on the landing, I took a good look around at the place, drinking it all in, as who knew when I'd be back. Then I looked down at a young officer on the landing below talking to a middle-aged, long-serving inmate in front of him, who was merrily vaping away.

Mum's the word

A young officer didn't turn up for work this morning, so a quick phone call was made, basically telling him to get his arse in to work unless he had a bloody good reason not to. Nearly an hour later, he arrived, explaining that it wasn't his fault he was late. It was his mum's fault, because she hadn't got him up.

Confidence

A new young officer started to ascend the stairs today, but two inmates were blocking his way onto the next landing. When he approached them, the inmates turned away, with their backs now facing the officer, and wouldn't let him pass. The officer repeatedly and politely said, 'Excuse me, please,' and when they ignored him for the final time, he turned and went back down the stairs. The inmates laughed and they knew they had the measure of him now.

This might sound amusing in isolation, but it stores up trouble and can cause big problems down the line.

Recently, another young officer with less than six months in the job was always getting a hard time. Inmates would drag their heels, refuse to bang up, go missing, make him wait, ignore him and generally give him the runaround – until they wanted something. Then they would offer him a deal. 'Do this for us, Guv, and we'll give you a week's amnesty. We'll leave you alone and won't get on your case.' It was completely ceding power to the inmate, and you can't have that. No one's saying you need to rule with a rod of iron, but a bit of backbone and assertiveness should be chiselled in stone for the job description.

Did you hear the one about the open gates in prison?

During the exercise period today I heard via the radio that they were about to move a vehicle through the exercise yard. Normal practice was to clear the yard and inform control once it was done. I went down to help clear the yard and was shocked when I saw the three gates from the wing to the exercise yard wide open.

Normally, once the inmates are out of the wing and on the exercise yard, the officer tells the control room how many inmates are on the exercise yard. Once the gates are locked, that's it, your roll goes into the control room, confirming your numbers, and the gates don't get unlocked until exercise is over. You can't have the gates open and free flow of movement, because you would never know how many inmates were on the exercise yard.

I asked an officer why the gates were open and I was told that it was so the men could come and go as they pleased, as it saved having to open and close the things.

Bemused and slightly confused, I asked, 'What's the roll?' He didn't know. I then said I'd give him a hand clearing the yard. 'Why?' he asked. I explained that a vehicle was coming through (he was blissfully unaware because he had turned his radio off while he was talking to an inmate). 'Oh, we don't bother with that,' he said. 'It just goes through!'

Gates should only ever be opened one at a time and the open one was supposed to be monitored. To have more than one gate open, a vehicle coming through and no knowledge of the number of inmates was a comedy of errors, to which he had added the perfect punchline by turning off his radio.

Tea round

The wing cleaners were supposedly out cleaning today, when one of them said to the NEPO, ''Ere, Guv, you couldn't do us a favour and make us a brew, could you?' Off the NEPO went to make the inmates tea and coffee.

The basics

We were failing in the most basic aspects of our job, and failing regularly. A librarian heard banging and knocking coming from one of the workshops during her lunch break today. Knowing the workshops were supposed to be empty over lunchtime, she called the control room and reported it. An officer was despatched to investigate, only to find an inmate in the supposedly empty shop. The inmate explained that the others had all gone without him. The scary thing was that not one person had noticed he was missing. Inmates were supposed to be counted in and out of the workshops or anywhere else and then counted back onto the wing. Those two counts were not done.

This was hot on the heels of another incident that happened during teatime a few days ago. We banged up the wing, counted and signed for the roll – confirming the fact that all of the inmates were locked up and the numbers were correct. We left the wing and made our way to the gate, but we never got there, as we received a call to return to one of the wings. An inmate was walking around one of the landings on a different wing because he hadn't been locked in his cell.

A quick check to see who signed for that landing revealed that it was a fairly new officer with just a few months in the job. The worrying thing was that when she was told of her monumental cock-up, she simply said, 'Oh, I must have forgot!' The inmate could have assaulted her or planned this, but she really didn't seem to understand the seriousness of what she had actually done. It was frightening.

Radio ga-ga

An inmate brought a new officer's radio into the office today, stating that the officer had left it when he went to talk to someone. Radios, like keys, should be attached to the officer at all times, but when challenged about it he simply replied, 'I wondered where it was.'

A lone inmate

An alarm bell went off in the visits area today. Visits had finished and everyone had returned to the wings, so the place should have been empty. When the responding staff arrived, they were met by a thoroughly pissed-off inmate, who informed them: 'They just fucked off and left me on my lonesome.' Again, this inmate wasn't missed, which meant that the fundamental basics of the job weren't being followed. Worse, they weren't deemed important.

The failure of staff to sweep the area and make sure the place was secure and clear of inmates suggested that the new-generation prison officer was oblivious to the basics of the job. It was, I'm afraid to say, a disaster waiting to happen.

Fellatio: a screws' debate

A small and seemingly insignificant incident took place today that seemed to sum up the ridiculous situation the prison service had found itself in. A new young officer with just three weeks in the job had found a couple of inmates indulging in the ever-popular pastime of fellatio. The officer, shocked and slightly perturbed at such an appalling sight, came into the office explaining what she had seen and asked if she should nick them.

Fortunately for her, the three officers in the office were all hugely experienced, each with over twenty-five years in the job, so it was only ever going to be a unanimous, 'Yes, nick 'em.' Unfortunately, the young, newly promoted CM had other ideas and informed the new officer that she couldn't place them on report, because, 'What the men do in their own rooms is private and if it was consensual, there's nothing you can do about it!'

The old-school screws were, it seemed, now out of touch with the ways of the modern prison service. But they weren't about to take it sitting down from an over-promoted, sycophantic CM with limited experience but higher rank, so a rank versus experience culture clash began.

The officers put across the point that any sexual activity was against the prison rules, lest it be a form of bullying, rape, payment, debt clearing and the like. The CM retaliated by stating that consensual sex between inmates wasn't against the rules. The experienced officers condemned the act; the CM condoned the act; and the new officer was just confused by the whole thing.

It turned out that this grey area of prison blow jobs was, in fact, not as grey as we had first thought. Oral sex between inmates was allowed. However, it was apparently only allowed in a double cell and only if those inmates were doubled (in other words, shared the cell), and they must be in a 'relationship'. It must also be consensual and only at certain times of the day, preferably when officers weren't doing a roll check. A simple yes or no would have been so much easier. How the hell could anyone know all that for sure? We left the topics of anal intercourse and mutual masturbation for another day.

The last day

Today was my last day in the job after twenty-eight years of service. It was just a shift like any other, starting at 07.30 and ending at 13.15, then I walked out with no fanfare, no goodbye. I wouldn't expect any different, of course, and longer-serving officers than me have left without so much as a handshake or a 'thanks for your service'. But it does make you wonder whether management couldn't show a bit more appreciation towards their staff. For my part, I was glad to step out of those gates and know I wouldn't have to set foot in there ever again.

The way management dealt with inmates and their problems was a world away from how officers on the 'shop floor' dealt with inmates. It's easy to find solutions, solve problems and cast judgement from the relative comfort of an office.

I'd been at Albany for four and a half years, and in that time I'd seen the number one governor of the prison on the wing twice; each occasion amounted to less than fifteen minutes, which, over fifty-four months, is roughly seventeen seconds a month. Yet, we were constantly bombarded with instructions on how to do our job.

Officers received emails every day that were 'cascaded' down to us. Today, I had nine emails in a three-hour period from the same person. Not one of them was relevant to me. By the end of the shift (five hours) I had twenty-four irrelevant emails addressed to me. Often, we would get the same email three or four times, which would suggest that one simple task was being needlessly repeated. And the emails were full of a language that only someone in the know understands: fashionable management phrases, acronyms – some of it was just gobbledygook.

The prison service relies on people skills. I was told during my training at Newbold Revel that it was my personality that would get me through. Yet, the man managers are often invisible. Seemingly aloof and unapproachable, they are the ones who apparently know how to manage the wing, a wing that they rarely see, feel, smell or experience.

As I finish my time in the prison service, I feel much like the convicted inmate does. I've done my time and served my sentence. Every long-serving officer hates the job and what it has now become. They all, without fail, want out. It's a dangerous, unpleasant and thankless task. Hopelessness and despair in a prison were once the over-whelming emotions experienced by the convicts, but that has now been turned completely on its head. We, not the inmates, struggle and despair with the futility of it all, and it's made so much worse by the large number of 'decision makers' sitting behind a desk who are making such a mess of it all.

Yet, speak to the inmates and you'll find that they are happy. The irony isn't lost on any of us. 'Doing a bit of bird ain't too bad,' they'll say. Many are reluctant to 'be on the out', and it's not hard to see why. PlayStations, duvets, healthcare, dental work, education, gym facilities, photocopying done on request, meals three times a day, newspapers delivered. Even internet shopping is made easy with the new breed of officer more than happy to look online for the inmate, printing out details of size, colour and price of the item the inmate requires. It saddens me that as my time here comes to an end, this once public service has now very much become the prisoners' service.

CONCLUSION:

From Discipline to Care

Does prison work? Far cleverer people than me know the answer to that question. People with university degrees and a distinction in an '-ology' or two. People who know how to read spreadsheets and flow charts, and interpret reams of statistics, though are unlikely ever to have set foot on a wing for any length of time.

Apparently, there are four main purposes to any prison: retribution, deterrence, rehabilitation and incapacitation. The definition of retribution is 'punishment inflicted on someone', and yet we are repeatedly told that inmates aren't to be punished; they are to be rehabilitated and helped to see the error of their past criminal ways.

Deterrence is 'the action of discouraging through fear of the consequences' and yet there are few real consequences for many prisoners, beyond an inability to mix with the public.

Rehabilitation is 'the action of restoring someone to health or normal life'. But 'normal life' for a lot of inmates is a life of crime and as the reoffending statistics show, rehabilitation simply isn't working.

Through incapacitation, we supposedly 'prevent the individual from committing future crimes'. Yet, committing crimes in prison is the norm, a way of life. It's made worse by policymakers, who end up condoning it by always taking the soft option rather than the hard-line approach.

Whether or not prison works is all a bit too clever for me and above my pay grade, but then most things are above a prison officer's pay grade. However, the simple indisputable fact is that in 1993, the UK prison population was 44,552; in 2018, it was 83,295.* That one simple fact must surely speak for itself. When inmates are happy and undeterred about doing a 'bit of bird', when inmates see prison as a lifestyle choice or business opportunity, surely something must have gone very wrong.

When you see the same prisoner for the umpteenth time, doing his umpteenth sentence, and when you add to that the erosion of staffing levels, particularly since 2010 thanks to the government's austerity measures that saw something like 7000 prison-officer jobs cut, combined with the increase of assaults on staff,† and the answer seems clear: the prison service is broken.

And it's not just the statistics that bear this out. On the ground, the morale and pride of staff are at rock bottom. The 'appeasement policy', as we longer-serving screws call it, appears to be the only thing holding it together: give the inmates everything and let them want for nothing is the theory. It's a slightly flawed theory, if only because inmates will always want more, especially that which they can't *yet* have.

The public service side of the prison service was slowly being broken up. Trades officers, carpenters, electricians

---

* UK Prison Population Statistics. House of Commons Library. July 2019.

† In my prison alone it has gone from fourteen in the year 2015/16 to thirty-five in 2016/17 to sixty-two in 2017/18 – along with, in 2016, an increase nationally of 40 per cent from the previous year (Safety in Custody Statistics Bulletin, England and Wales. Ministry of Justice. September 2016).

and the like were responsible for maintaining the prison until a huge contract was awarded to Carillion Plc in 2015. Carillion Plc were seemingly in way above their heads and couldn't cope – their performance was roundly criticised – and this multinational facilities management and construction company promptly went to the wall at the beginning of 2018. This led to an administrative nightmare for staff on the ground trying to get even the simplest maintenance job or repair done. The Ministry of Justice was then forced to *renationalise* the facilities management side of things by taking on 1000 Carillion staff in a new company.

Fortunately, the powers that be understand and appreciate the fact that the system is broken and have come up with a radical cost-effective, problem-solving solution: rebrand the service!

So now prison wings become house blocks or house units; cells have become rooms. Officers are now to be known in paperwork as case workers; senior officers as offender supervisors (OS); principal officers as custodial managers (CM). Inmates are no longer inmates or numbers but equals to be addressed as 'residents' – Mr or Miss. Ironically, it is the officer who is now reduced to a number, an epaulette number, and is waiting for his sentence within the prison to end.

Our old-fashioned job title of discipline officer, suggesting that we were there to impose some form of discipline as opposed to helping the poor unfortunates in our care, was now a thing of the past – and with the word discipline gone, it felt like any actual discipline went with it. It definitely felt like I joined the service as a discipline officer and ended my service as a full-time care assistant to the needy.

Hospital officers are likewise a thing of the past. By 2006, the NHS had taken over and the no-nonsense 'scab lifters' were replaced by super-caring nurses who treated the inmate as a patient, rather than as a prisoner who requires treatment like the no-nonsense scab lifter did. The NHS Care UK nurses who work for the prison are capable but officially not allowed to do the simplest of procedures, such as stitches, checking for overdosing (we get a lot of inmates saying they've taken too many pills), changing catheters and the like. Instead, inmates often get taken to the outside hospital for these simple things, which is a time-consuming and more expensive way of doing things. These NHS professionals are patient, empathetic and a lot more caring, willing to talk to and listen to the inmate, all of which is great for the inmate but not for the rest of us.

Time and again, inmates have been late for work because they have been collecting their morning medication at the treatment hatch and talked for so long with the nurses, while a long queue moved slowly. The NHS staff are employed by the prison service to take care of and treat the inmates; they are not obliged to deal with an injured officer. Fortunately for us, however, these super NHS staff have always treated us when needed.

And then there's the paperwork. The endless reams of it, the countless boxes to tick. The powers that be would like to know everything about an inmate at the touch of a button, not realising for one minute that if an officer actually sat at a computer writing, reporting and justifying an inmate's behaviour, he would be tied to the computer for an entire shift. Only the bare essentials make it to the computer, but a lot of information that would be useful to have on there isn't because there just isn't the time. When you actually do get to sit down to log on to a computer, a governor will invariably walk into the office and say, 'Why are you not on the landing?'

Angela Levin, in her book *Wormwood Scrubs: The Inside Story*, says, quite rightly:

> I believe that the administration and bureaucracy in prisons should be urgently addressed. Instead of employing vast numbers of civil servants to create ever increasing convoluted and verbally inflated prison service orders, individuals should be employed who can write or edit in a concise, easy to understand way that will shorten them without affecting security or safety. This will help lighten the bureaucratic burden on staff and cut down on repetitive form filling which takes up so much time.

The introduction of computers, we were assured, would cut down on the paperwork. In the outside world, computers are used to make a difficult job easy and save time. Only in the prison service could computers be used to make easy jobs difficult and take twice as long to complete.

The governors, in fairness, realised that an officer's paperwork was time-consuming and distracts an officer from the all-important landing work, so they finally had the good sense to reduce the number of inmates per officer ratio and limit each officer to six inmates, from more like double this number before, which was far more practical. Unfortunately, they overlooked the fact that a wing full of a hundred inmates would require seventeen officers, and there weren't enough officers to make this a practical solution. Another seemingly good idea that landed on the scrap heap.

In the last couple of years, there have been belated efforts to address the staffing shortages in prison, but the type of officer now being recruited is very different to those employed at the beginning of my career. The modern prison service has decided that the recruitment of ex-military types should be phased out – sort of. University graduates with their undoubted superior intellect would make a far better prison officer than some ex-squaddie who can stand his ground, not be intimidated by violent offenders, and who can speak the language of many of the inmates. No, graduates are the future. Who better to deal with the career criminal, the serial killer, the habitual burglar from the local estate who settles disputes with violence and intimidation rather than reasoned debate?

When I joined the prison service, I was thirty-two years old and I was considered a bit young for the job back then. Today, many officers are joining at the age of twenty to twenty-one. This isn't intended to be a rant against the many young 'snowflakes', but they haven't had the time to develop the kind of life skills that I feel are essential to the job. The ability to articulate and reason is wasted and meaningless on a criminal whose main form of communication is intimidation, physical violence, self-harm or silence. Graduating from the school of hard knocks is a necessary qualification for the job. A lot of new officers in their naivety hope that their overconfidence and their gentle, non-confrontational approach will prevail. It won't. The streetwise career criminal with a master's degree in manipulation will always have the upper hand.

Dealing with aggression, whether verbal or physical, on a daily basis is draining for anyone, and surely a better balance of staff would better enable the staff to manage the demands of the inmates. Graduates and the new breed of officers have their place, of course, but so, too, does the no-nonsense screw, who can enforce the prison's rules with unflinching discipline. After all, who do you want covering your back when you're about to go in to do a C & R on an eighteen-stone hulk of a violent offender?

In 2018, there was finally some belated recognition of this. The prisons minister made an announcement that owing to the lack of experienced staff, the prison service was asking for retired officers to rejoin. The old-school discipline officer was, it seemed, exactly what was needed on the landings. These are the same old screws that the service wanted rid of and gave substantial pay-offs to do so only a few years previously. And, while the government made a big deal about recruiting 2500 new officers in 2018, they made no mention of the fact that the number of officers had dropped by some 7000 since 2010. I'm no maths whizz, but even I can tell that doesn't add up.

At the very beginning of this book I said that the prison environment was 'so alien, so oppressive and so frightening' that it must, I had reasoned, be 'like entering the underworld, a place of misery, evil, hate and condemnation . . . quite literally the end of the road.' Now, after being on the inside for twenty-eight years, I realised that I was very wrong indeed.

Prisons no longer act as a deterrent. They seem to me to be little more than places of learning and rehabilitation – a cross between the Open University and the Priory. Had Dostoevsky been writing his classic book *Crime and Punishment* in modern-day Britain, he would have to call the book *Crime and Rehabilitation*. But rehabilitation clearly isn't working either, as the repeat offending statistics demonstrate.★

When I think back to my first week in the job – the inmate with the cut throat and the claret-covered cell, the officers and their, 'You're on your own', sink or swim attitude, with the near loss of the wing – I wonder, was the training back then better? Were the criteria tighter, the selection process more thorough?

The POA – the Prison Officers Association – seem to agree. They lay out the role of the prison officer as follows:

> In the last twenty years the role of a prison officer has changed from that of a supervisor or guard to that of a multi skilled manager of offenders. Officers have to fulfil the role of teacher, trainer, welfare officer, agony aunt, listener, enforcer and supervisor. Their work continues to evolve to ensure the demands of the service are met and re-offending reduced.[†]

They go on to state that:

> . . . it is fundamental that they are all trained and empowered to deliver the work that is demanded of them. Unfortunately, in the last twenty years the training for officers has been eroded and is inadequate to properly train staff for the professional work required of them

---

★ See: <https://www.gov.uk/government/collections/proven-reoffending-statistics> [date accessed: 13.04.20]

† See: https://www.poauk.org.uk/index.php?the-role-of-a-prison-officer

The POA rightly state that:

> The prison service as a career is not as attractive as other public services but it could be with the right makeover. The salary is too low compared to the police and fire and rescue services.

We don't warrant the same kind of recognition that the NHS or police do, and few of us mind that. We accept that we're part of a secret service, the public service no one wants to hear about. But a fair wage for what is at times an unfair job surely shouldn't be too much to ask. Offering lower salaries inevitably reduces the calibre of the potential candidate. In real terms, year on year, prison officers have effectively had a pay cut. It's this undervaluing of a very difficult and dangerous job in the eyes of the paymasters that really rankles.

We have understaffed prisons with undertrained officers, in a job undervalued by the general public and the Ministry of Justice alike. Management are faceless bureaucrats, strangers to the day-to-day realities of working on a wing and apparently more concerned about the welfare of prisoners than staff. We are seeing an increase in assaults on officers and an epidemic of spice plaguing the wings. It is, I'm afraid to say, a perfect storm, and it's the staff on the front line who will have to weather it. Make no mistake, it will take something major to finally sort out the mess our prisons have become, and I fear that it's only a matter of time before something happens that will see prisons plastered over the front pages again. And remember, the only time prisons ever make the front page is when something truly bad happens.

When I sit here and reflect back on my time as a prison officer, I feel saddened that a job that was once a proud discipline, a public service, has been decimated and destroyed. I'm grateful to have done my time in prison and leave a free man, relatively unscathed by my sentence, but I have many friends and valued colleagues still working inside. To them – and to all of you working in prisons up and down the land – I wish you well. Stay safe and thank you.

ACKNOWLEDGEMENTS

A lot is written about the British prison service without much actually being known about it. It's the one public service that appears to be shrouded in secrecy, literally behind closed doors. *A shambolic service with corrupt staff. A violent, overcrowded holiday camp, filled with drugs, mobiles and bullying.* These are the headlines. But this is just a fraction of the reality.

I have written this book in the hope that a fraction more of the real story behind the headlines can be seen. I have so many people to thank, starting with those many colleagues and friends who I have had the pleasure to work with throughout my time as an officer, 90 per cent of whom are professional, hard-working and honest, and who don't get the positive recognition they deserve.

I'd even like to thank the inmates, who made the job challenging, interesting and at times rather scary.

I would like to say a huge thank you to Robert Smith, whose encouragement and enthusiasm for the book got the thing off the ground; Vicky Eribo at Orion, who took a leap of faith and got the ball rolling; and Steve Burdett, who had the unenviable and mammoth task of editing a manuscript that was, at best, rough and ready.

And finally, to my wife, Marilyn, who has been there for nearly forty years for the before, during and after – and who encouraged me to put pen to paper. Your love and support are truly appreciated.

GLOSSARY:

Prison Slang and Official Terms

ACCT: Assessment, Care in Custody and Teamwork
(a document that is regularly signed to say a suicidal
inmate is alive)

ASO: Acting Senior Officer

Association area: a recreation area of sorts, where inmates
socialise and play pool during their association time

Back cell: an isolated cell at the back of the Seg unit

Bang up: locking-up time

Block: the Seg Unit

BOV: Board of Visitors

Bootneck: Royal Marine

BWVC: Body Worn Video Cameras

C & R: Control and Restraint

CC: cellular confinement

Chokey: the Seg Unit

CID: Criminal Investigation Department

Claret: blood

CM: Custodial Manager

Compound: large exercise area and also a main thoroughfare for the inmates going to and from work

DST: Dedicated Search Team

ED: Evening Duty

Fab Check form: form filled out prior to a cell being
occupied

Fish: tool for cutting ligatures

Flyer: go home early after shift

HCC: Healthcare Centre

Hooch: illicitly brewed alcohol

Hotel unit: hospital officers

IEP: Incentives and Earned Privilege

Jail craft: picking up little fluctuations in behaviour, reading body language, feeling the atmosphere

Kanga/Kangaroo: screw

Kilo unit: Seg unit officers

KPIs: Key Performance Indicators

Labour movement board: board used to mark each inmate off as they went to work

LBBs: Locks, Bolts and Bars (now AFC, Accomodation Fabric Check)

Left-handed letter: letter issuing threats against prison officer

Mike unit: classes and education

MQPL reps: reps Measuring the Quality of Prisoners' Lives

MSL: Minimum Staffing Level

NEPO: New Entrant Prison Officer

Nicking: putting an inmate on report

O1: radio call sign for Principal Officer

Obs book: wing observation book, for recording anything of interest that has happened on the wing

Omertà: the code of silence

Oscars: principal officers

Ones (twos, threes etc.): denotes the landing, with ones being ground floor, twos the first floor and so on

OS: Offender Supervisors

OSG: Operational Support Grade

Package: cat A prisoner

Pad mate: cell mate

PEIs: Physical Education Instructors

Peter: cell

PNOMIS: Prison National Offender Management
Information System

PO: Principal Officer

POA: Prison Officers Association

Poncing: borrowing or acquiring

Potting: throwing faecal matter

PWU: Protected Witness Unit (Supergrass Unit)

SARU: Segregation and Rehabilitation Unit (formerly
Seg unit)

Scab lifter: hospital officer (in pre-NHS days)

Screw: prison guard

Seg unit: Segregation Unit

Shitting up: dirty protest

Shop instructor: oversees prisoners working

SMT: Senior Management Team

Spin: search

Stored prop: inmate's property that is stored in the reception area of the prison

SSU: Special Secure Unit

The net: radio network

TOIL hours: Time Off In Lieu

Tornado: riot-trained officers

VICS reps: reps for veterans in custody support

Victors: governors

VP: Vulnerable Prisoner

Wrapped up: prison speak for physically restraining an
inmate, an officer on each arm applying wrist locks and
an officer controlling the head

Zulus: dog handlers

Uniformed staff by rank:

PO: Principal Officer, the highest uniform grade (later
   CM: Custodial Manager)
SO: Senior Officer (later OS: Offender Supervisor)
Officer: basic-grade officer
OSG: Operational Support Grade (supporting role not
   dealing directly with inmates)